Adrian Vincent w~~...~~ for twenty-seven years, becoming managing editor of IPC's educational magazines. He is the author of many books on art and antiques, novels and true crime. His most recent book is *A Gallery of Poisoners*. He lives in Norfolk.

Also by Adrian Vincent

Fiction
End of a Summer's Day
The Squirrel Cage
Song at Twilight

Art and Antiques
Antiques for All
Victorian Watercolours 1) Rural Life
2) Victorian Children
19th-Century Maritime Watercolours
A Hundred Years of British Traditional Painting
A Companion to Victorian and Edwardian Artists

Non-fiction
The Long Road Home
The Face of Evil
Fatal Passions
A Gallery of Poisoners

Children's Books
The Bellamy Book of Nature
The Book of Transport
A Book of Days
Life on the Home Front (1914–1918)

Killers in Uniform

Adrian Vincent

HEADLINE

First published in 1994
by HEADLINE BOOK PUBLISHING

First published in paperback in 1994
by HEADLINE BOOK PUBLISHING

10 9 8 7 6 5 4 3 2 1

ISBN 0 7472 4316 6

Printed and bound in Great Britain by
Cox & Wyman Ltd, Reading, Berks

HEADLINE BOOK PUBLISHING
A division of Hodder Headline PLC
338 Euston Road
London NW1 3BH

CONTENTS

CONTENTS

CONTENTS

THE
BEAST OF BECCLES

Aircraftsman Arthur Heys was known to be very much of a family man, with no record of accosting women, which made his actions all the more surprising when, on the evening of 8 November 1944, he accosted Winifred Mary Evans, and strangled her after having brutally raped her, leaving her body in a ditch to be found the following morning. The murder took place near Beccles, in Suffolk, where he was stationed.

The first Scotland Yard heard of the murder was when a call came in from the Suffolk Constabulary, telling them that a young woman had been found dead. The case was handed over to Inspector Ted Greeno, who set off immediately for Beccles, where he wasted no time in making his way to the scene of the crime where the girl's body lay in a ditch under a sheet of tarpaulin. The girl had serious abdominal injuries. Her liver had been ruptured and her private parts were also heavily soiled with blood. She had not died from her injuries, but had been suffocated to death by having her face pressed down in the snow-covered ditch where she lay.

After the Inspector had examined the body it was taken to Beccles Hospital, where a detailed autopsy was carried out. Afterwards, the Inspector went to a nearby Italian POW camp, where for the rest of that night he examined the prisoners. When he had finished his hours of cross examination, Greeno realised he would have to look elsewhere for his murderer. The task before him was enormous. There were countless thousands of troops in the area, all of whom had to be screened, and there was also the possibility that the murder had been committed by a civilian, which added to his problems.

He learned that the murdered girl had gone that night to a dance at an American camp, and had returned from it in the company of a friend, Corporal Margaret Johns. As it was very dark that night, Johns offered to see her back to her billet, but the offer was politely refused. Margaret Johns was therefore probably the last person to see her alive.

Before turning in that night, Johns made her way to the women's bathrooms, and was surprised to find a man reeling about inside. That man was Heys.

'What are you doing here?' Corporal Johns said angrily. 'These are the women's toilets.'

'I'm very sorry,' the airman said apologetically. He lurched blindly against the door. 'I'm afraid I'm very drunk. I wonder if you would be kind enough to point me in the direction of the RAF camp.'

The man seemed harmless enough and Corporal Johns accepted his story without any alarm. Taking him outside, she set him on the path for the RAF camp and then went to her own billet for the night.

When she learned the news the following day, she quietly got in touch with Heys' CO. When he questioned Heys he was somewhat surprised and reassured when Heys freely admitted to the incident in the WAAF's toilets, but denied anything else happening that night. However, the CO was still not entirely satisfied, and ordered Corporal Johns to be present at the next pay parade. But Heys got wind of what was happening and lined up with the Rs instead of the Hs. This clumsy attempt to conceal his identity only served to make matters worse for him when it was discovered. Inspector Greeno, who was also present at the pay parade, then obtained Heys' RAF tunic and trousers, which had recently been sponged and pressed. There was some mud left on the tunic, and the trousers still had some reddish stains on them, despite the attempt to remove them. Although the evidence was tenuous, Greeno still considered he had enough to make a case, and the Director of Public Prosecutions agreed with him.

Heys was arrested. Sitting in his cell, he looked silently at the floor for some minutes before speaking to Greeno. 'I have been thinking,' he said. 'I can't think what evidence you have to connect me with it. Can't you tell me?'

'No,' said Greeno. 'Not at this stage. For more information, you will have to await the trial.'

But Heys still persisted.

'I wonder what clue they have got,' he said later on to the officer who was guarding him at the time. 'Chief Inspector Greeno took six hairs from my head. If any of them are found on her clothing, how am I to prove he didn't put them there? If there is any evidence against me, it has been faked up by the police.'

This was quite untrue. Greeno had not placed the hairs on the murdered girl's clothing. Instead, he had gone to Heys' house in Colne, Lancashire, where he had collected some hairs belonging to Heys from his wife. He passed them on to forensic as a matter of routine, just in case they later found some matching hairs on the corpse.

As it happened, the Director of Public Prosecutions had already decided to discard the evidence of the hairs as not being substantial enough to support his case. Heys did not know this at the time and proceeded to dig his own grave with an act of incredible stupidity.

Before the trial, Heys' CO received an anonymous letter purporting to be from the man who had killed the WAAF:

Will you please give this letter to the solicitors for the airman who is so wrongfully accused of murdering Winnie Evans? I wish to state that I am responsible for the above-mentioned girl's death. I had arranged to meet her at the bottom of the road, where the body was found, at midnight. When I arrived, she was not there. I waited some time, and decided to walk down towards the WAAF quarters. Just before I reached this I heard a voice and stood close to the hedge. I heard footsteps. It proved to be an airman. I don't think he saw me. I then saw someone I recognised was Winnie. She said I should not have come down to meet her, as the airman ahead was drunk and had lost his way . . .

How did the writer of the letter know that Heys was drunk and had lost his way? Only two people could know that;

Corporal Margaret Johns and Heys, awaiting trial in prison.

This farrago of nonsense, printed in block letters, in an attempt to conceal the identity of the writer, was, of course, written by Heys himself in a last futile attempt to put the blame on some unknown assailant. Instead, with that letter he sealed his fate just as surely as if he had stood up in court and proclaimed his guilt to all and sundry. One might say that if he had not written the letter, he might well have got away with it.

He spent some time in Norwich prison before he was sent to attend his trial, which was held in January 1945 at Bury St Edmunds, where he was found guilty and sentenced to be hanged.

Basically he was not an evil man but, like so many men before him, he took to drink, which all too clearly he had been unable to hold, with tragic consequences.

It must have been a bad moment for Greeno when he confronted Mrs Heys, and even worse for her when she realised what had happened down in Suffolk. To face the fact that her husband was a rapist and a brutal murderer was almost too much for her, but fortunately she had her children to give her moral support in the dark days that lay ahead. Even so, it could not have been easy, having to go through the rest of her life branded as the wife of a convicted murderer.

A DRINK
BEFORE DYING

Neville Heath, or Lord Dudley, as he liked to call himself
from time to time, was a twenty-eight-year-old RAF officer
with oodles of charm which most women found immensely
appealing. He was also a sexual sadist, who liked to lay
about him with a riding whip, given the opportunity.

He joined the RAF in 1937 at the age of twenty, and in no
time at all he was dismissed for being Absent Without
Leave. Within three months he was caught obtaining credit
by fraud. Six months after that he was sent to Borstal for
housebreaking and forgery and for ten other minor
offences. This inauspicious start to his career was only the
beginning.

When the Second World War broke out he joined the
RASC and was soon considered such good officer material
that he was given a commission almost right away. He was
then posted to the Middle East, where he immediately
began issuing dud cheques, for which he was again
arrested, and this time shipped home to South Africa. He
escaped from his captors at Johannesburg, where he joined
the South African Air Force. It was not long before he
married and had a son, and he was promoted to the rank

of captain. If anyone thought that he had settled down at last to a life of respectability with his wife and child, they were very much mistaken.

At the end of the war his wife filed a petition against him for desertion, and it was at about this time that he was court-martialled, this time for wearing unauthorised decorations, and was dismissed from the service.

He returned to England in February 1946 and within a few weeks he was caught posing as Lord Dudley, while again wearing decorations to which he was not entitled.

While waiting for the court's verdict he registered at the Pembridge Court Hotel, Notting Hill Gate, on Sunday 16 June. He signed the register in his own name, but could not resist adding the rank of Lieutenant Colonel. He was accompanied by a young woman who claimed to be his wife.

From all accounts it was a highly successful evening, and the young lady left happy with the way everything had turned out. It was only later on, once he had got into his stride and murdered Margery Gardener and his life had become part of the daily newspaper headlines, that she realised just how lucky she had been in escaping from Heath with her life.

About a week later he picked up Margery Gardener, a twenty-three-year-old film extra. After drinking most of the night away at the Panama Club in Kensington he took her back to his hotel for the night. The next morning the maid went into the room to find Heath had already gone. But one of the beds was still occupied. The room was in half darkness and it was difficult for her to see anything at first, but when she did draw back the curtains and throw off the bedcovers it was to see the body of a naked girl bound by the ankles and with her arms folded behind her.

The body was covered with a number of lash marks and both nipples and breasts had been bitten and torn. Although the maid could not have known at the time as she ran screaming from the room, the girl's vagina had also been slashed with some sort of knife so that she had a seven-inch cut running from it. The injuries were appalling, and could only have been made by some sort of madman.

'Done with a knife I should think,' said the pathologist who had been summoned to the scene. He looked quickly over to the fireplace, 'Or with something like that poker standing in the corner over there.'

Her body was still warm when it was examined and it was established that the savage, brutal thrust into her vagina had not been the cause of death, as her face seemed to indicate asphyxia.

Heath had meanwhile slipped away to Bournemouth, where he had booked into the Tollard Royal Hotel and registered under the name of Group Captain Rupert Brooke. It was obviously the first name that had come into his head when he registered.

A few days later, while strolling quietly along the promenade, he picked up Doreen Marshall, who was enchanted by this charming young Group Captain. She happened to be staying at the Norfolk Hotel, so he took her to lunch there and then to dinner at his hotel that evening, where they sat talking until midnight.

He wanted to see her back to her hotel, but she demurred and ordered a taxi. We do not know what happened the rest of that evening, but we do know that her naked and mutilated body was found the next morning in Branksome Chine. Again, the breasts had been grossly bitten and the nipples chewed off, as well as being slashed with a knife. She was already dead from a haemorrhage of the carotid artery when he slit her vagina with a rough instrument. Once again, Heath's sadistic lust had got so far out of control that he was able to commit the most appalling mutilations on his victim without a qualm. Nor did he ever show any remorse at what he had done.

Two days passed before Doreen Marshall was discovered to be missing and her absence duly reported to the police. Detectives interviewed the manager of the Norfolk Hotel, who could throw no light on her absence, beyond saying that he thought she had dined with a Captain Brooke, whom he believed was staying at the Tollard Royal Hotel.

The police immediately went to see Heath, who later identified Doreen's photograph at the police station.

Later on, he swaggered into Bournemouth police station prompt at the appointed hour of 5.30. He confirmed that it was she with whom he had dined the previous night, and stated that after he had seen her back to her hotel he had gone out for a quiet stroll along the front. Heath talked fluently and easily to Detective Constable Souter as he lounged against the counter, but Souter was vaguely worried. He was sure he had seen this man before. Then it came to him. Only days before he had seen a photograph of the man wanted for the murder of Margery Gardener.

'What's your name?' he asked casually. 'It wouldn't happen to be Heath, would it?'

Heath blenched and then quickly recovered himself.

'Of course not,' he said at once.

He shivered suddenly. 'I must go back to the hotel for my jacket,' he said.

'Don't worry,' the Detective Constable said easily. 'I'll have it brought round for you.'

When the policeman returned with the jacket, Detective Constable Souter went through the pockets in front of Heath, and found a railway cloakroom ticket.

'I think we'll take a look at this,' Souter said cheerfully. 'You don't mind, do you? But of course you don't.'

The ticket led them straight to an attaché case that contained a leather-bound whip. It was evidence enough to have Heath arrested and put on trial for murder at the Old Bailey.

The case attracted more attention than most when it opened in September 1946. It was such an open-and-shut case the defence had only one line open to him. After all the damaging evidence against Heath had been presented, J. D. Casswell got to his feet to make his final address to the jury:

'Surely it must be evident to everyone in this court that this man is as mad as a hatter. Absolutely insane – a maniac,' he began. Heath sat through all this with apparent unconcern, seemingly quite confident that he was going to get away with it, even though at one stage a senior medical officer at Brixton Prison had been called to the witness box to say that in his opinion Heath was quite sane. If he still had any hopes of getting away with his life, the evidence of the senior medical officer of Brixton must have surely put an end to them on that score. But no, he remained cool and confident to the last, and it was not until the jury of ten

11

men and two women returned with a verdict of guilty that his self-confidence seemed to leave him. It is surprising that the jury took as long as it did before coming to its verdict.

Sentence of death was passed on him and it was at this point that something of his old jaunty manner returned. Springing smartly to attention, he wheeled around between his two guards and then disappeared from the view of the public.

At least Heath showed a certain amount of style immediately prior to his execution. When he appeared in the execution shed, exactly three minutes before the execution was due to take place, he came forward at the same time as the prison governor who was walking towards him.

'Heath. I presume you would like a whisky,' he said.

'Yes,' Heath said, grinning. 'You had better make it a double while you're about it.'

Even in a case of this nature where the evidence points us squarely at the accused, there remain some unanswered questions. Why did Heath behave so correctly towards his wife, when their marriage did not endure and he was divorced for desertion? Though he was a man of uncontrollable sexual appetites, there was no question at any time of him behaving in an unseemly manner towards her. Why did he not try it on with her as he had done with Doreen Marshall and Margery Gardener?

There is also the matter of the young girl who happily survived the night with him. Why was she not slaughtered after having been put through the usual ritual with Heath's whip? It might have been because she shared some of his sexual tastes and enjoyed being whipped. The unexpected

12

pleasure of finding a willing partner probably delighted him so much that he did not feel impelled to inflict injuries on her as he had done on the others, who no doubt felt only disgust when they realised what his intentions were – a fact that could only have brought out the worst in him.

Heath was hanged in Pentonville Prison on 26 October 1946.

HE KILLED
HIS MOTHER

His real name was John Donald Merrett when our story begins, and he was living in Edinburgh with his mother. He was only eighteen at the time and was a broad-shouldered youth with a forbidding manner towards anyone who crossed him.

He was born on 17 August 1909, the son of an electrical engineer whom his mother had met while travelling to New Zealand. He had been a large, handsome child from the beginning and was christened John Donald.

From the outset he was doted on by his mother. When he was only three years old Mr Merrett changed his job for one in St Petersburg in Russia, but the bitter climate did not suit either the child or his mother, who took him away to Switzerland where he was given into the charge of a governess.

At the outbreak of the First World War Mrs Merrett asked her husband whether she should go back to England. He replied, 'Stay where you are.'

After the war, during which Mrs Merrett spent much of her time nursing wounded soldiers, the family went to London, where Mrs Merrett worked with the Ministry of

Food. Meanwhile, however, the marriage had broken down, and when John Donald was twelve years old she went back to New Zealand in the hope that she would be able to find her husband. Like so many wartime husbands, Mr Merrett seems to have disappeared completely, and so Mrs Merrett came back to England and took a cottage near Reading and sent her son to Malvern College, where he remained throughout the year of 1925. He then went to Edinburgh, where his mother was now living, where he studied for some time at the university. He showed a natural facility for study, and came top in a number of subjects. One way and another a glittering future seemed to lie ahead of him with a job in the offing in the Diplomatic Service on which he had already set his sights.

Unfortunately, he had also had time to see less respectable side of the city. Unknown to his mother he had become friendly with two dance hostesses from one of the local dance halls, who had encouraged him to leave the university in favour of the more raffish life that could be found outside.

He had taken to the seamier side of life in Edinburgh like the proverbial duck to water. He had also acquired some expensive tastes on the way, which he didn't have the money to sustain. He solved the problem by the simple expedient of stealing one of his mother's cheque books and then forging cheques from it. From such small beginnings was to come an incredible life of crime which was also to embrace murder. But his mother was no simpleton and it was only a matter of time, therefore, before he was found out.

Mrs Merrett was meticulous about financial matters. She kept her money in three accounts, one with the Midland Bank, one at a branch of the Clydesdale Bank, and a third elsewhere.

It was not easy to defraud a woman of such careful habits, but he managed it for some time before the Clydesdale Bank wrote to her saying:

> We think it well to advise you that cheques have been paid by us on your account, which makes it overdrawn by the amount of £6.11s.3d.

The letter came as a severe shock to Mrs Merrett, who was always careful to keep herself in credit. Even so, to shoot herself was a reaction which was somewhat over the top.

Later that day the housekeeper heard a shot and ran into the lobby where she found Mrs Merrett lying on the floor and bleeding profusely from a bullet wound. A pistol which Merrett had bought for himself earlier in the week lay on the floor beside her.

Merrett accompanied her to the Royal Infirmary, and on the way there he voiced the opinion that his mother had shot herself, an opinion that the police seemed to share. Not for one moment did they suspect that she had been shot by her own son. After all, why should they? Everybody in the area knew Mrs Merrett as a hard-working woman who got on well with her son.

Several days after she had been admitted to hospital a letter was received at the Infirmary from the Edinburgh police which read as follows:

I have the honour to inform you that Mrs Merrett now detained at No. 3 Ward at the Royal Infirmary is a prisoner, and is now charged with attempted suicide, and I am directed by the Police Constable to ask you to inform the Lieutenant on duty. When the accused is finally discharged, arrangements are being made to take her into custody.

Although Mrs Merrett lived for another fortnight, during which time she was conscious and lucid, she could remember nothing of what had happened. As a result, therefore, Donald Merrett went scot free.

Soon afterwards Inspector Fleming of the Edinburgh police went through the flat where the incident had taken place. In the process he discovered two letters from the Clydesdale Bank intimating that Mrs Merrett's account had become overdrawn. This merely strengthened his belief that this was a case of suicide.

There were still a few sticky moments, however, for John Donald Merrett before he was reasonably sure that he was in the clear. There was, for instance, the matter of Inspector Fleming who had continued his inquiries for some time before finally giving up on the case.

Even then he was far from being out of trouble. The Procurator Fiscal of Midlothian had also been busy. He had gone through all the statements carefully and examined the cheques, which were later sent off to a handwriting expert in London who proved that no fewer than twenty-nine of them had almost certainly been forged by Merrett.

The police now concluded that Mrs Merrett had been murdered by her son and a warrant was issued for his arrest. He was taken into custody in Edinburgh where he was charged and locked up in a cell for the night, but if anybody thought that was the prelude to the end for him, they didn't know Merrett, who throughout his life was to show an extraordinary ability for getting out of tight spots.

We have an example of how he got away with it this time by trying to evoke a verdict of Not Proven. His defence counsel, Mr Aitcheson, in his final address to the jury said: 'I say with the utmost respect that if you send this lad out into life with a verdict of Not Proven, with the stigma that implies, you are taking a terrible responsibility on your shoulders. I therefore claim from you a verdict of Not Guilty on both charges.'

These were brave and magnificent words, and they certainly did the trick as far as John Donald Merrett was concerned. He was sentenced to twelve months' imprisonment.

Prison was not a pleasant place to be in, but at least he was alive. After the shock of having to put on the shapeless grey prison clothing, he was able to reflect just how lucky he had been in escaping the death penalty. He did not enjoy prison life with its dreary daily routine of having to sit for hours at a time sewing mail bags, but his education stood him in good stead with the prison guards, who treated him with more respect than most of the other prisoners, who were mostly hard cases with little or no education. As a result of his erudition he was able to worm his way into a number of soft jobs which all helped to make prison life more tolerable.

One way and another his time in jail passed smoothly enough and he came out, after serving only eight months of his sentence, with his ego not too severely bruised.

Once back in the outside world he made no serious attempt to find a job. Always the opportunist, he took advantage of his leisure by roaming the city and picking up girls, and generally having a good time with them until the money granted to him by the Public Trustees ran out.

In due course he married a good-looking young girl named Vera Bonnar and at this time changed his name to Chesney. Under the influence of Vera, who was a staunch Roman Catholic, he took up religion. With Vera he went on a little holiday, driving through the border country, where they stayed for the night at the ancient town of Berwick-on-Tweed. He opened an account with the local bank and was given a cheque book. Once that came into his possession he was soon up to his old tricks again, issuing cheques that bounced.

He then promised Vera an engagement ring as a measure of compensation for not having bought her one before. The jeweller welcomed them both with open arms, and mesmerised by Chesney's open manner, he accepted a cheque in payment for the ring. Within minutes the ring was pawned at another shop and the money went into Chesney's pocket. Vera was so besotted with him that she went along with everything, even sacrificing the ring to make Chesney some easy money. Finding yet another jeweller's on the same day, he purchased a bracelet which also quickly found its way to another pawnbroker's.

Emboldened by success, Chesney tried to make another fraudulent transaction and attempted to cash a cheque in a large store. The manager became suspicious and quietly informed the police, who came at once to the store and after a few pertinent questions, arrested the couple and took them away.

Chesney was charged with attempting to obtain goods by false pretences. This time he had no defence to offer, and he was sentenced to six months' imprisonment and three months to run concurrently. Less than eight months after his release he was again back in prison. The magistrate let Vera off with a warning. After he had done his time, Chesney moved with Vera to Appledram, near Chichester, where he began mixing with some of the naval officers who lived in the area.

It was then that he decided to take up boxing. He went down to the gymnasium and stripped off for a bout with anyone who was willing to take on this fourteen-stone boxer. As most of the men present were around the nine-stone mark, no one was keen to take him on. Eventually, however, someone took up the challenge and slipped into the ring. After inflicting several blows on Chesney's prominent nose, his smaller opponent was smashed to the ground by Chesney, who went on quickly to apologise. 'Sorry, old man,' he said. 'It's always the same; I just don't seem to be able to pull my punches when the occasion demands it.'

A few weeks later he was selected to meet an opponent more his own weight at the Connaught Hall in Portsmouth. This time, faced with a more worthy opponent, Chesney cabled an apology to the boxing ring, saying he had to decline the date owing to his wife's objections. It was not that he was a coward in the ring, but he had no desire to

21

subject himself to the possibility of being bested, to the detriment of his ego.

Soon afterwards the Chesneys moved to a twenty-roomed house in Weybridge, complete with swimming pool and considerable acreage. He was helped to obtain the house by his mother-in-law, Lady Menzies, who moved in with them. Immediately prior to the move he and Vera adopted a little girl of two months, and together with the child that had been born to them earlier, they all settled in to a life of respectability. He was even a paid-up member of the golf club.

All this cost money which he didn't have, even allowing for the helping hand of Lady Menzies who chipped in from time to time whenever he became short of cash, which was often. How then did he manage, you might well ask.

For a number of weeks all went well. By now he had acquired a yacht, and at the helm Chesney cut a dashing figure with cap set at a jaunty angle. He did not always take the family with him, and when he went out alone it was to engage in a little gun smuggling, mostly around Poole, where he had a number of useful contacts. Whenever he was at home he made a point of attending most of the naval parties, generally with Vera in tow.

Quite often Vera was glad when he went off alone. A man well known to everybody for his womanising, he was the cause of many a violent row in the house, often in front of the children. Not that it was any different when they accompanied him abroad, where Chesney seemed to have an endless supply of shop assistants or waitresses available.

Soon he became a well-known figure abroad, where he mixed with prominent businessmen and stayed at their villas while the business deals were set up. All in all, Chesney was leading a glamorous life of easy money.

It was at about this time that he met a dark-skinned girl called Miriam. This affair was more serious than any of his others had been. But after two weeks of hectic lovemaking he had an offer to smuggle some gold and diamonds from Tangier across to France and England, and being a man to whom money came first he reluctantly said goodbye to her and never saw her again.

Once he had completed his business, Chesney decided that it was time he made his peace with his wife. Accordingly he suggested to her that the two of them should make a trip to Rome, where they would pay homage to the Pope. Vera was overjoyed at the prospect, and there followed a brief period of harmony as the couple made their way to Rome, stopping at Capri on the way. Despite all his womanising, there is no doubt that Chesney was genuinely fond of Vera at this stage.

It was now 1938 and, glamorous as his life was, Chesney had become bored with it and was planning to turn his vessel into a gambling ship. It became just that, with Vera slinking around the tables in the latest gowns from Paris.

Meanwhile, war clouds were gathering over Europe; something which dismayed most people, but not Chesney, who was delighted with the prospect. When 1939 came and Poland was attacked, Chesney flew back to his home in Weybridge while Vera found a house in one of the residential areas of Ealing. The house was in St Mary's Road, and was a fairly modest affair after what they had been used to. Nevertheless, the family settled into it comfortably while Vera went out to earn a little extra money at a nursing home for elderly people. There seems to be no reason as to why they should have decided to lead separate lives, unless it was because Chesney was once more chasing women, which was most likely. However, they did get together again when the Chesneys joined the ARP in Ealing. This didn't last long as he went off to join the Royal Navy after having been offered a commission.

Ronald Chesney joined the Royal Navy on 5 January 1940, and did his initial training in Glasgow before being sent to HMS *King Alfred*, which was berthed in Hove, Sussex, as a Sub-Lieutenant. Once again his breezy good humour and his enormous appetite in the mess became something of a byword. The posting was welcomed by Chesney for two reasons; one, it meant that he could get away from Vera's watchful eye, and the other was that he was hoping to get stationed in the Mediterranean where he hoped to run across some of his old smuggling friends.

In 1941 he was given charge of motor-gunboat 92. At the end of 1940 he had already been warned to prepare himself for a posting in the Middle East, and at the beginning of the following year he was given command of the schooner *Kheir el Din* anchored at Alexandria.

His war was probably no better or worse than most, and most of the time involved getting in and out of Tobruk without running into the Germans. On one occasion, however, he was taken prisoner by the Italians, but once again he was lucky, inasmuch as he was repatriated in exchange for a sick Italian sailor.

After the war he was offered a posting which he immediately accepted and was sent to the German

Admiralty Headquarters at Wilhelmshaven. For once he behaved himself, except for an affair with an eighteen-year-old girl named Gerda Schaller whom he had rashly promised to marry after he had divorced his wife. He took her with him on a trip to Paris where he was unlucky enough to run into Lieutenant Ronald Basnett of the Military Police, who knew of his past activities. 'I believe you are Lieutenant Commander Chesney,' he said formally. 'I would like you to come along to police headquarters.'

In the event Gerda was released while Chesney was put under arrest and taken to the army barracks in Hamburg, where Gerda came every night to see him. The court sentenced him to six months' imprisonment for smuggling, after having taken into consideration that he had already spent six weeks in custody. He told Gerda that he was going to serve out his sentence in England, and on 10 November he arrived at Wormwood Scrubs, where he seems to have spent his time bragging about his wartime exploits.

When he came out of prison, Gerda was waiting for him at the gates. With her he went back to Germany, where he involved himself in the black market.

This time he went through a mock marriage for which he had acquired the services of a seedy Frenchman who had gabbled his way through the ceremony and then had quickly taken himself off.

From the beginning Gerda had been suspicious. 'Tell me the truth, Ches. Are we really married?'

'Of course,' he lied. 'The service was quite legal.'

Afterwards they had set off for Algiers, where they had booked into a third-class hotel. Later Chesney had gone out alone into the town where he gambled recklessly and lost most of his money. The next day he went out gambling again and ended up with nothing in his pocket. The result was that Gerda had to sell a piece of jewellery to pay the hotel bill. Clearly the time had come for them to leave Algiers which had proved to be so unlucky for Chesney. That night he asked Gerda to search about for anything of value. Gerda ended the evening minus a watch, two small diamond brooches and a diamond ring, which he put away in a cigar box. Before they had a chance to make a sale they were met by a policeman, who accosted them in the street the following morning.

'My name is Commissar Guyot of the Sûreté,' he said, raising his hat. 'Perhaps we should have a little talk. It would be more tranquil in my office.'

They accompanied him and Chesney said, 'I'm sure you know me.'

'Indeed I do,' Guyot said coldly. 'I think we had better start by seeing both your passports.'

He looked at the name in Gerda's passport, which was certainly not Chesney, although he had told her that the name had been changed on it when they were married. Guyot passed it back without comment and then looked at Chesney's. 'You are a very well-known man, not only in Algiers, but also in Paris. Now would you let me have a look at your pistol?'

Chesney dumbly handed it over.

'Now your firearms certificate.'

Chesney knew that he had no such certificate. When he made no move to produce it, Guyot said, his voice hardening, 'If you have anything of value to be said on this matter you may say it in front of an examining magistrate.'

26

On his way to the car, Chesney asked, 'What about the young lady with me?'

'I don't want her,' said Guyot. 'She can go.'

'It looks as if I might be going to prison,' Chesney whispered to Gerda. 'By tomorrow I shall know how long I shall be away. As soon as I am settled in I will write.'

Chesney had been right. As a result of being arrested he was ultimately charged and sentenced to four months' imprisonment, and fined 150,000 francs for making a fraudulent entry into France, and for smuggling. Considering the circumstances, he got off lightly, though it has to be said that he did not enjoy being in a French jail, where hygiene was lax and of little importance, and the warders tougher than in Britain.

When he came out he found Gerda waiting for him, and together they went back to a life of crime. He was planning a trip to the Riviera when he received a letter from Vera, asking for money. 'That bloody woman,' Chesney fulminated. 'She's already had thousands out of me, now she wants more.'

'Send her some money,' Gerda said. 'After all, we don't want her coming over here for help.'

Reluctantly, Chesney sent her some money, but this did not prevent her from arriving on his doorstep one evening while he was in the middle of a party. Sighing, Chesney pulled out his wallet. 'How much?' he asked wearily.

After he had given her some money to tide her over, for the first time they seriously discussed divorce. It was clear that whatever had once existed between them lay only in the past.

'Goodbye,' she said to Gerda in conclusion. 'I hope you

will be happy with each other. Just don't trust him too much, I beg you.'

Chesney was soon in prison again, this time in England, where he was sent to Pentonville for his black-market activities. After he left the prison he aimed to set up an import–export agency, and in this venture he had an unexpected piece of luck. One evening he met a pretty blonde girl named Sonia who lived with her parents in a suburb of Cologne, where they kept a greengrocer's shop. She was twenty-four, while Chesney was forty-two. He told Sonia's parents that he was an important businessman. The parents were impressed and he was allowed to operate his business from their shop. Despite the fact that he was now looking much older, Chesney courted Sonia with his customary charm, living with her now under the name of Milner.

Running short of cash as he was, he began developing homicidal plans for Vera, whose very existence threatened his future. Once more Vera came over to see him, and again he brought up the question of divorce.

'I have now decided that I will never divorce you,' she told him. 'So please don't bring it up again.'

On 24 April Chesney was again in court, and this time was sentenced to six months' imprisonment at the Lewes Magistrates' Court, where he heard himself described as a professional smuggler since 1947. He served out his time in Wandsworth Prison, where he finally decided that Vera must go. He had already committed the ultimate crime of murdering his own mother. Now he was about to murder his wife.

He had originally intended to use the services of Ronnie

Burgess, who was to be paid the sum of £1,000 for doing the job. In the event, Burgess decided not to do it and offered it around his prison mates at double the price. Rather surprisingly he received no offers to do the job, and it was then that Chesney decided to do it himself.

After taking Sonia back to Germany, where she was looked after by her parents, he went to stay with his wife and her mother, who were now running an old folks' home at Ealing. He stayed there until the rows over a possible divorce made it so unbearable that he had to leave.

The next day he shaved off the moustache he had acquired, smoothed out his hair and then bought himself a pair of spectacles. Meanwhile, he had been reading up on the trial of George Joseph Smith, who had been tried for the murders of three women in their baths. He decided that Vera would go the same way.

Brooding over the case he then went back to Germany to see Sonia. After only the briefest of stays he returned to England, whereupon he took Vera out to dinner and then to the pictures.

The next morning the maid arrived at the nursing home as usual. Taking Vera's tea in, she was surprised to find she was not in her bedroom. The maid then went into the bathroom, where she found the naked body of Vera lying in the bath. Soon after that she came across the body of Vera's mother. Unlike her daughter, she was still fully clothed. One of her stockings was around her neck and it was obvious she had been bludgeoned to death with a coffee pot which lay on the floor nearby.

All this was evidence enough to lead the police to Chesney. An alert was put out for him, and on 16 February he was found in a wood just outside Cologne with his brains shot out. As for the two women who had survived him, poor Gerda, whom he had deserted months ago, had made a new life for herself, though she did go to Chesney's funeral. The last Mrs Chesney, however, had to live on, haunted by the knowledge that the man she had loved was a murderer three times over.

HE KILLED
FOR LOVE

Sergeant Mick Emmett-Dunne was well known for being a hard case who was liable to pick a fight with anyone at the slightest provocation – such was his reputation at the army camp at Duisburg, Germany. It was hardly surprising, therefore, that he had few friends. One of the few exceptions was 'Tich' Watters, who was a good friend to everyone. A thick-set Yorkshire man, he was the life and soul of any mess party, and seemed incapable of making trouble with anybody. He was a seemingly happy-go-lucky man without a care in the world, and it therefore came as somewhat of an unpleasant shock to all when it was learned that he had been found hanging by the neck in No. 2 barracks over the stairs at No. 3 entrance. The body had been discovered by Emmett-Dunne, who had cut him down.

The next day the body was examined by a newly appointed and vastly inexperienced pathologist named Alan Wommack, who was nevertheless self-assured enough to state without hesitation that the injuries were consistent with someone who had committed suicide, a statement which was accepted without question by the

31

army, although there was an absence of any motive.

The case remained a nine-day wonder until after Watters had been buried, when everything went back to normal and the whole incident was quickly forgotten. Soon afterwards it became obvious that Emmett-Dunne and the wife of the dead sergeant were seeing too much of each other, considering the circumstances.

Tongues began to wag, and this unfortunate situation lasted for some six months before Emmett-Dunne returned to England, to take up a new post at Catterick. Mrs Watters also returned to England, where she quietly married Emmett-Dunne. News of the marriage soon filtered through to Duisburg, and once more the gossiping tongues began to wag. One of those who heard of the marriage was Emmett-Dunne's own half-brother, who was also stationed at Duisburg at the time.

He was so perturbed by the news that he went to the local police station with the information that Emmett-Dunne had told him that Watters had become very depressed and that he had been contemplating suicide. This was so unlike Watters that with hindsight it sounded more like a prelude to murder than anything else. The half-brother had felt impelled to report it, but the local police did not take the statement seriously, as Watters' body had already been exhumed when the gossip had reached the army.

More as a matter of routine than anything else, the authorities duly reported it to the army in London, who supplied the best available pathologist, Dr Camps, who in due course conducted an examination and announced that Watters had not died by strangulation, but by a blow to the throat. The pathologist was asked if it could have been a light blow. 'Oh, yes indeed,' said Dr Camps, 'and even that could be enough to kill him.'

By this time Emmett-Dunne and the former Mrs Watters were living in army quarters in Taunton, Somerset. Following Dr Camps' startling statement Emmett-Dunne was arrested, and in due course appeared at the magistrates' court at Bow Street. It was then that he made a plea that as a citizen of Eire he could not be tried for a crime committed on foreign soil. The magistrate accepted the plea and the military police immediately moved in and he was taken into custody to Germany, to appear before a military court of seven officers, presided over by a brigadier. What he hoped to gain by this move is not clear, unless he expected the army would look on his case more favourably than a civilian court.

First, Mrs Emmett-Dunne was brought over from England to swear that there had been no love affair between her and Emmett-Dunne while her husband was alive. 'He danced with me perhaps more than with the other women, but we were not in love,' she said.

Throughout the trial Emmett-Dunne behaved abominably towards everyone, including those trying to help him. He was insolent to counsel and adopted a hectoring tone to all, as well as bawling out the witnesses who did not agree with him. As far as Mr Griffith Jones for the prosecution was concerned, the case was a straightforward one with Emmett-Dunne killing Watters with a commando-like blow which had broken his Adam's apple. As for motive, it was clear enough that Emmett-Dunne had lost his temper and lashed out, killing Watters.

Ronald Emmett-Dunne, the half-brother, had then come forward to make a statement to the effect that Emmett-Dunne had killed Watters and had appealed to him (in vain, as it happened) to make the death look like suicide. This statement caused something of an uproar in the court and seemed to seal the fate of Emmett-Dunne.

But Griffith Jones had not finished yet, there was still more to come – evidence that would threaten to prove Emmett-Dunne's guilt. The findings of the court had already established that Watters had not died by hanging, but from a blow to the throat, which had struck him at the most vulnerable part of his body and caused almost instant death. Griffith Jones had already established that Emmett-Dunne had been stationed with the Irish Guards, where he had been taught to administer the sort of blow that had killed Watters in seconds.

'You thought then that Emmett-Dunne had killed Watters because he wanted his wife?'

'Yes,' replied Ronald Emmett-Dunne.

'That made him a murderer then?'

'Yes, indeed.'

The fact that the killing was an accident did not help Emmett-Dunne much, and he was found guilty of murder mainly because the prosecution still claimed that he had killed his victim intentionally.

When he saw the way the trial was going, Emmett-Dunne admitted to the killing, claiming that he had killed Watters in self-defence. According to him, Watters had accused him of living with his wife while they were out on exercise.

'I told him he was talking out of the back of his head, and

said he was being ridiculous,' Emmett-Dunne told the court.

'Did Watters' manner seem strange?'

Emmett-Dunne claimed that he had a pistol in his hand which he had taken from his coat pocket. 'The gun was loaded and I could see there were three or more rounds in the chamber.'

'What then?' asked Curtis Bennett, the defence counsel.

'I raised my arm slowly,' said Emmett-Dunne.

'What were you going to do?'

'I was hoping to gain possession of the revolver and take it from him.'

'Listen to this carefully,' said Mr Curtis Bennett. 'Did you intend to kill him?'

'No, sir,' Emmett-Dunne said in a low voice.

There were so many inconsistencies in the story that it was not altogether surprising that the court found him guilty. He was sentenced to suffer death by hanging. He decided to appeal, as was his soldier's right, and presented a petition to the Queen for mercy, but it was turned down. He was saved from hanging, however, because capital punishment had been abolished in Germany.

He was taken to England to serve out his term of imprisonment in an English jail, and that is the last we hear of him until 1964 when he emerged briefly to attend the divorce from his wife, when it was noticed that he had gone completely grey.

THE MAN WHO WANTED
TO CHANGE HIS WIFE

There is no doubt that by the time he was thirty-seven, Sergeant Marcus Marymont was already past his best. His sullen, podgy face, set in lines of permanent disappointment, did not make him look like a promising lover, and though he had once been attractive enough to lure a marriage partner, he was only too well aware of his shortcomings. Lonely and unhappy, he was all too susceptible to the charms of someone else. That someone was Mrs Cynthia Taylor, who was anxious to be rid of her husband in exchange for another.

The Sergeant was stationed at Sculthorpe in Norfolk and was to meet Mrs Taylor at a dance he had gone to in Maidenhead; and it was unfortunate for him that they should get together and begin sleeping with one another. Within a few months Marymont had become besotted with her and was yearning to be free of his wife.

This unhappy state of affairs lasted until June 1958, when his wife was admitted to the base hospital at Sculthorpe suffering from acute stomach pains. When she died the following day the authorities immediately ordered an autopsy, ignoring Marymont's protests when he tried to prevent it being carried out. It was then that it was discovered that she had died from arsenical poisoning.

From the beginning Marymont's attitude did not encourage much sympathy. Instead of appearing upset by the death of his wife, he was far more inclined to discuss with all and sundry the sexual problems he had been having with her. Already the whole business was beginning to look suspicious to say the least.

At the trial he waited anxiously for the evidence of Dr Albert Cook, who had been stationed at Sculthorpe camp and whose patient Mrs Marymont had been until he left the camp. During that period it transpired that she had gone to see him several times with severe vomiting attacks.

'Could these attacks of vomiting have been as a result of arsenical poisoning?' he was asked by Major Lewis, acting for the prosecution.

'Speaking with hindsight, they could well have been,' Dr Cook said.

Only on one occasion did Marcus Marymont get any show of sympathy from the court, and that was when Major Karr, acting for the defence, asked the nurse on the case if the Sergeant had seemed very upset by his wife's death.

'He sobbed by the bedside,' said the nurse. '"What am I going to tell my little boys?" he kept asking. He must have sobbed for a full ten minutes,' she added.

But when it came down to it her comments did not really help his case. He might well have been upset by the fact that his sons were now deprived of a mother, but he had still shown very little grief over her death. The case against

Marcus Marymont began to look very black, though what counted against him most was his attitude towards his wife. Nor was the evidence of Dr Camps of much help to him. First of all he stated that beyond all doubt the findings so far pointed to arsenical poisoning.

'Of course, there are several ways it could have got into the body,' he admitted.

'Perhaps she could have eaten rat poison by mistake,' suggested the defence counsel hopefully.

'I know of no rat poison on the market which contains arsenic,' Dr Camps told him. 'All we know for certain is that a lethal dose was given to the dead woman probably twenty-four hours before her death.'

Mrs Taylor was then asked to give evidence. 'How long have you known the accused?' she was asked.

'Two years,' she said simply. 'Once I got to know him well, I saw him on a regular basis about twice a month.'

'Did you know he was married?' she was asked.

'No. I thought he was divorced.'

'Did you ever discuss any marriage plans?'

Mrs Taylor nodded. 'He promised to marry me when I got my divorce at the end of the year. Probably in December.'

Captain Ellis Dufficy, the assistant prosecuting counsel read out to the court a statement which Marymont had made, in which he stated that they had been married in 1943. The statement then went on to say: 'Ours was a happy marriage until my return from Japan in 1954. After that we did not seem to have the same relationship. Soon after we were transferred to a base in Texas, where we did seem to get into a rut. I then transferred to Britain in 1956 and we

39

got an apartment in King's Lynn. We then found a house, but it was not up to American standards and my wife was not very happy.' The Captain put the document down. 'What then?' he asked Sergeant Marymont.

'In the July of that year I visited a club in Maidenhead where I became acquainted with Mrs Taylor whom I visited a number of times. She was married but separated from her husband, who I believe treated her badly. Later on I told her I was divorced but would marry her. We later became intimate. This went on for some time, until now in fact, when I was arrested,' the Sergeant testified.

'Have you anything to add to that?' Major Lewis asked him.

'Only that my wife eventually found out about the affair because I had been foolish enough to leave a letter to Mrs Taylor lying around. I told her I would try to give her up. She was still very upset about the affair and talked of moving out of the house. It was about this time that she suddenly began being ill.'

It seemed on the surface of it that Marymont had been honest about the affair, but only because he knew it was just a matter of time before it all came out. He was therefore only admitting to something that would soon become common knowledge. Major Hugh McManus, the Medical Officer at Sculthorpe said that he had seen Marymont the same day that his wife had died and he had not seemed unduly upset by her death. As can be imagined, the statement did Marymont little good.

Mrs Theresa Dunning, the wife of one of the sergeants at Sculthorpe said that Mrs Marymont was a good housewife who was devoted to her family and was also a religious person. Cross-examined by Major William Karr, acting for the defence, she admitted that earlier in the year Mrs Marymont had been taken ill and had complained of stomach pains.

He also got two cleaners from the base to admit that arsenic was kept in the laboratory and was a potential death hazard to anyone unwise enough to use it.

Major Lewis then returned to Marymont's morals.

'Are you in love with Cynthia Taylor?' he asked.

'During the past two years I would say I was in love with her,' Marymont admitted.

'Would you say deeply in love?'

'No, I would not,' Marymont said. 'I would say that I was in love with Mrs Taylor, but I was not deeply in love with her.'

Major Lewis then went on to another tack. 'Do you admit having a sexual relationship with Mrs Taylor?' he asked.

'Yes, I do,' the Sergeant said calmly. 'I have already admitted it.'

'Would it be fair to say that you promised marriage to Mrs Taylor?'

'No. We merely discussed it on the basis of her obtaining her freedom.'

'Did you have any love and affection for your wife and family?' he was then asked.

'Yes, I did.'

'Yet you spent Christmas of 1957 with Cynthia Taylor, leaving your wife and children alone in a foreign land.'

Marymont had to admit that this was true.

Major Lewis then asked, 'Did you ask for a divorce?'

'No, I did not ask for a divorce,' Marymont said.

'Would it be fair to say that when it comes down to it, Mrs Marymont was determined to keep the family together?'

'That is true,' Marymont said.

'Sergeant, did you go to Cynthia Taylor only four days after the death of your wife?'

'Yes, I did,' agreed Marymont in a low voice.

'Don't you think that your children might have needed you during this difficult time?' Major Lewis asked him coldly. Although he did his best to sound impersonal, it was clear that he did not have a very good impression of the accused.

'Did you make plans for your marriage to Cynthia Taylor now your wife had gone?'

'I'm afraid not,' Marymont said regretfully.

At this stage nothing had been definitely proven beyond the fact that his wife had died from an overdose of arsenic, and that a motive of sorts had been discovered in that Marymont had been having an affair at the time. None of this was hard evidence though, and it was not until Mrs Gertrude Marymont arrived on the scene that the case began to perk up. Mrs Marymont, the mother of the accused, had been summoned from California to give evidence, and on the stand she reminded Marymont that his wife had already written to him earlier in the year, telling her that she had been suffering from serious stomach upsets, which seemed to imply that Marcus Marymont had been dabbling with poison even at this stage.

There was also the evidence of Major G. L. Fletcher, Chief of the Intelligence Unit at Sculthorpe, who gave evidence to say that there had been a time when he had become very concerned about the health of the sergeant, who was worrying himself sick as to whether he should spend Christmas with Mrs Taylor or with his family.

Major Lewis continued his cross-examination of Marymont: 'Am I right in assuming that according to your original plan she would have been Mrs Marymont by now instead of Mrs Taylor?'

'No, that is not correct!'

'But did you not say she was fully expecting to become your wife?' asked Major Lewis, affecting to be slightly puzzled.

'That was because she was not aware of my marital situation,' Marymont said, looking uncomfortable, as well he might. If nothing else, Major Lewis was establishing the fact that he had been a first-class heel in his relationship with Cynthia Taylor. 'I did say, though,' he went on, 'that I would adopt her son, Chris, but as Mrs Taylor was married, my solicitor advised against it. I would like to say at this point that I have never entered a shop in Maidenhead asking for arsenic. Nor have I ever had arsenic in my quarters.'

This wrapped up the case before the court went into session to consider its verdict. But first there was an impassioned speech from Major William Karr, who drew attention to two letters which had been read to the court.

'Those two letters show a cooling in the affections of Mrs Taylor towards Sergeant Marymont,' he said. 'They were two letters from people who now had no particular affection for each other. I would therefore submit that if you have a girlfriend, and that is motive enough to convict a man of murder, then God help the greater portion of our society, because we know that sort of thing exists today, and it certainly does not create the motive for murder in every instance.'

The prosecuting counsel did its best with what was, after all, insubstantial evidence. Captain Ellis Dufficy, the assistant prosecution counsel, called Marymont 'a cool, calculating egotist'. 'The person that would carry out this type of murder is intelligent, cool and calculating. If Marymont does not fit into this category, then no one does,' he concluded. To call Marymont intelligent and calculating was to make a statement bordering on the absurd. If he had shown any sense, he would never have caused such a fuss about having an autopsy carried out. Nor would he have shown such a callous display of indifference over his wife's death.

In many respects the case turned out to be something of a farce in that there were occurrences which should never have taken place and were illegal in an English court of law. In the first place, no English judge would have allowed certain questions to have been put to Mrs Taylor, which could have been prejudicial to her pending divorce, and incidentally caused harm to Marymont.

As it was, he was sentenced to a term of life imprisonment which he was to serve at Fort Leavenworth in Texas, his home state rather than in England. He appealed against the sentence but this was turned down, and he was duly shipped out to begin his imprisonment.

In the beginning of 1959 Marymont wrote to Mrs Taylor proposing marriage. Mrs Taylor wrote back saying she would be pleased to marry him once her divorce was through. Her divorce actually went through in the latter part of 1959, but we do not know whether or not she finally married Marcus Marymont. Common sense may well have prevailed once she had got over the shock of hearing from him.

THE STRANGE CASE OF
GENENE ANN JONES

Genene Ann Jones, who was to become one of America's most infamous killers, was born on 13 July 1950 in San Antonio, Texas. Unwanted by her parents, she quickly became the adopted daughter of Dick and Gladys Jones, who already had four adopted children. Although San Antonio had now become a sprawling, noisy town with its own barrio where thousands of Mexicans lived out their lives, she grew up quietly enough in it with her four siblings, near the Mission of San Antonio de Valero, better known to the thousands of visitors who came to it as The Alamo, the shrine of no less a hero than Davy Crockett, who had died while defending its blood-stained walls against the notorious Santa Anna, whose reactionary policies had eventually lost him Texas.

By the 1920s the city had become famous for its gambling joints. One of Dick Jones' main sources of income came from the gambling halls he ran, including the Kit Kat Club, which brought him in a surprising amount of money from the slot machines he operated. There is no doubt that Dick Jones was a larger than life character, who weighed in at sixteen stone and stood over six feet in his socks. He was a character that Genene admired for being an inspired self-promoter whose hearty laughter booming around the place was something of a tonic to everyone. It was therefore a great shock to her when he was struck down with terminal cancer at the comparatively early age of fifty-six.

The year of 1968 was something of a watershed for Genene, who announced her forthcoming marriage to Jimmy DeLany, a young man she had met a couple of years earlier at the Marshall High School.

The honeymoon had gone well enough, despite her mother telling all and sundry that the marriage was doomed to failure. For the first few months the couple spent most of their time together either playing cards or throwing parties where a lot of alcohol was consumed.

As for the husband, who was a car mechanic, he worked only when he felt like it, with the inevitable result that the couple were broke for most of the time.

When the war in Vietnam came, Jimmy DeLany joined the navy and was stationed in San Diego where he served out most of his time before he went home on leave, only to discover that his wife was being unfaithful to him. This all but put an end to the marriage, but they managed to struggle on together for some time, with Genene trying to establish a career for herself as a beautician. By now Jimmy was based at the US Naval Station in Albany, Georgia, where he was eventually joined by his wife. She bore him a son there, and the marriage survived until 1974, when it broke up and she was finally left alone at the age of twenty-three.

Her mother, with her dire premonitions about the marriage fully vindicated, unexpectedly came to her rescue by offering to look after Genene's child while she was out at work. It was at this point that Genene made life even more difficult for herself by having another baby. The father was purported to be Keith Martin, a gentle man who had majored in both French and classical music. He was also a homosexual who resisted all her attempts to have sex with him until he began sharing the same bed with her, with the result that she soon became pregnant, so the story goes, though it is just as likely she conceived the child through one of her other promiscuous encounters.

Their oddball relationship lasted until one day in 1976, when during a flaming row between them, Keith Martin made it quite clear to Genene that he had no intention of marrying her. She had not abandoned the idea of running a beauty parlour, but was now casting her eyes towards a career of some sort in the medical profession, mainly because she had begun to lust after every young doctor she encountered.

Genene went home to San Antonio, where her mother was overjoyed to see her, so much so that she was quite happy to foot the bill for a nursing course at the San Antonio School for District Nurses, where she graduated with 559 points – 200 more than was needed for a pass. Even though she was seven months pregnant a promising new career was opening up before her, and she had her mother in the background to help her bring up the child.

But in no time at all she was fired from the Methodist Hospital in San Antonio, and left under a cloud following a long list of complaints issued against her by the patients who had not liked her overbearing manner.

Being unceremoniously booted out of her first job does

not seem to have done her much harm. As with most cities, San Antonio was suffering from a shortage of qualified people to call upon, and she was soon in another job, working this time for the local Community Hospital, but she had to leave shortly after through no fault of her own as she had to undergo an abdominal operation. She was now twenty-eight and had decided to have no more children, electing to undergo a tubal ligation. She next found herself a job with the Bexar County Hospital. By modern standards it was a terrible place to be in, especially if you were a patient. The food was appalling, and there was even a shortage of instruments, with the result that the doctors often brought in their own, rather than risk having to deal with a situation where a patient was in need of an operation and there were no instruments to hand to carry it out. Once again she was fired in the April of the same year, for improper and unprofessional conduct.

One would have thought that as a two-time loser, with a reputation for being difficult to get on with, her career would have been at an end. But no, she was soon back at work, this time at the Robert B. Green Memorial Hospital, which in the main treated the city's poor, being on the West Side, near the Mexican barrio from where most of the patients came.

One of her supervisors was Head Nurse Pat Belko of the Pediatric Intensive Care Unit. She had taken her degree in 1955 and was a product of the old school who never argued with the doctors. She had risen to middle management by remaining in one place for most of her career, despite having taken six years off from work to look after her six children. Supervisors regarded her as solid and reliable. Now sixty-four, she was a pleasant moon-faced woman with a reputation for following the line of least resistance. The world is full of such people who have risen to a position of authority by the sheer volume of work they have done over the years. Genene was always solicitous and respectful to her, which may have accounted for Belko speaking so well of her.

Despite all the praise that was showered on her by Mrs Belko, Genene was hardly deserving of it. So far, she had failed to give a child the right dosage of medicine and had failed to carry out doctors' orders in a number of other instances. Her fourth medication error in twelve months obliged her to attend special classes in the administration of drugs. How she managed to survive this catalogue of errors is something of a miracle.

At Christmas time she went back to her mother, who had been looking after her children all the time she had been away. She returned to the hospital in January, where she quickly made a number of new friends and became familiar with the doctors who seemed to have appeared since the holidays.

In the spring of 1980 Dr James Lawrence Robotham arrived on the scene. He was thirty-three, a wiry, bearded young man who had had a great deal of experience with young children, and from the beginning, Genene put her best foot forward in an attempt to please him.

The Robert B. Green Hospital was not much of a place, and in those days it had no reputation whatsoever, but it must have seemed like paradise to the patients who had come in straight from the barrio where they were forced to live without any form of sanitation or even running water.

Even so, it was still no place in which any full-blooded American would want to work. Even as late as the 1960s it was labelled as a ghetto of Mexican 'children' who just liked to sing and dance and have a good time – this from the Mayor of San Antonio, who had only contempt for his Mexican population that was still being treated like dirt by almost everyone save an enlightened few. It was in this sort of atmosphere that Genene flourished.

But moves were afoot to change conditions, heralded by an announcement that in future Bexar County Hospital would charge what people could afford. 'There is going to be a universal kind of care,' stated the medical authorities. 'The same kind of care for those who can pay and for those who cannot.' In effect, all that happened was that the rich shopped around for their medical care, thereby avoiding having to mix with the Mexican population, while the poor continued to go to the Green. In fact, everything went on very much as before.

As far back as 1978, 80 per cent of the patients at the Green Hospital were Hispanic, and even today its Hispanic patients are still being treated with the same mixture of care and indifference.

In the same year it was decided to close down the Green Hospital with the result that Genene was transferred to the Bexar County Hospital's Pediatric Intensive Care Unit. Her first case there was a six-day-old little boy who had an often fatal disease. He was sent down to surgery and then came back to the ward and died. It was not the first time a child in her care had died, but this time she was quite upset; far more than on any other occasion, though why this should have been is not clear.

Apart from this lapse, Genene's natural talent for her work seemed to dazzle her superiors. Doctor Robotham was a strong disciplinarian who was quite merciless on the young doctors and nurses around him. The nurses in particular seemed to be his pet anathema, and when he arrived at the Bexar County Hospital they were the first to hear from him about any lax behaviour in the running of the wards. Rather surprisingly, considering her track record, Genene was not picked out for one of these attacks, and it was not long before she became one of his most trusted assistants.

Robotham had grown up among those to whom Albert Schweitzer, the famous doctor, was a revered figure, and he still harboured romantic dreams of following in his footsteps. When this had not materialised he had concentrated most of his energies towards the care of young children. He had sent the Chairman of the Intensive Care Unit a ten-page memo in which he stated that the hospital needed new equipment if it was to maintain its position in the field of medicine. When his memo was ignored, Robotham found an outlet by throwing himself more and more into his work.

Working together as often as they did, it was inevitable that Genene and JR, as she now called him, grew very close for a while. This meant she now had two superiors who could help her future – Head Nurse Belko and JR.

Since beginning her nursing career, Genene had been forced to rely a great deal on her aging mother, who had done an enormous amount for her by taking on the care of the two children while Genene was at the hospital. When it began to be too much for her mother to handle, Genene moved into an apartment near the hospital, taking her mother with her.

With her mother preparing all the meals for them while Genene tucked the children up for the night, the situation worked fairly well, though the youngest child, Crystal, began causing trouble because she had reached the age when she had become jealous of her brother. As for Genene, she was feeling more secure than she had ever been now that she was under Dr Robotham's care and patronage. Whenever she was accused of being his favourite she sent her critics away with a stream of abuse and bad language.

It was at about this time that she began to develop a whole series of symptoms, and then fell ill with a number of complaints, ranging from diarrhoea and vomiting to an acute attack of gastro-enteritis, as well as a whole host of imaginary complaints. Unable to find any serious problems save that of bronchitis, for which she was merely told to give up smoking forthwith, she was sent on her way.

By the early part of 1981 Genene was taking on far more work than she was capable of handling. She began asking for assignments to handle only the patients who were the most ill. The Charge Nurse on the shift was always an RN, and it was her responsibility to allocate the patient to a nurse she felt could handle the case. Most of the time Genene decided whose case she wanted to handle and duly put her name against the patient on the charge sheet. The nurse in charge hardly ever bothered to disagree with her decision.

When a child was seriously ill and died, Genene would

break down and cry over it as though the child were her own. After death, she would take the child to the cold room herself, often carrying the tiny corpse in her arms instead of placing it on a trolley and taking it down. Whenever the opportunity presented itself she would gladly assume the responsibility of taking dead children to the cold room and do whatever had to be done.

The last few months had in fact seen an enormous change in her personality. Where once she had been a burly vulgarian who had always been quick to dole out a string of obscenities at the slightest provocation, she had become much more subdued, and did her best to look after her dead charges until the parents arrived to see the body. 'After all,' she was fond of saying. 'We don't know for sure when the spark leaves the body.'

It was not until the death of a six-year-old child that anyone noticed anything seriously wrong. Already children had begun to die without reasonable cause. Only recently there had been the case of Patricia Sambrano, only three months old, who had died after a seizure following a routine inoculation administered by Genene.

This was by no means the first fatality, and doctors began to wonder what was going wrong. Was it possible that some instruments were being contaminated, or that perhaps some serious germ was running loose around the wards? When Christopher Hogeda also died, a thorough investigation was carried out. They even began looking at the charge sheets, when an interesting fact emerged. All the children had died while under the care of Nurse Genene Jones, and on the one shift.

Dr Robotham was called in to make a number of discreet

inquiries, but could throw no light on the mysterious deaths that were still occurring. Pat Belko was also called in. She had already heard some of the rumours flying around about Genene, and she immediately leapt to her defence, saying what a good nurse she was despite the fact that her manner was somewhat abrasive, which had undoubtedly upset a lot of people.

It was at this point that RN Suzanna Maldonado came briefly into the picture. The twenty-five-year-old nurse had taken a dislike to Genene, whom she considered nothing more than a loud-mouthed upstart. Among other things she compiled a list of patients who had died since the long string of deaths had begun. She went to Pat Belko with the information and stated that there was something very fishy going on. 'It looks really bad,' she informed Pat Belko.

Pat Belko was shaken by the news which she realised she could not ignore. She immediately sought out Dr Robotham and found him making up his notes for the day. On hearing what she had to say to him he had to agree that there would have to be an investigation.

The case was eventually handed over to Virginia Mousseau, the hospital's assistant director. After hearing the accusations against one of her nurses she made no further effort to handle the case, beyond telling Belko to make sure that all the proper procedures were carried out. Other than that, she did nothing to make sure that anything else was done concerning the cases.

Acting on his own initiative, Dr Robotham had taken the matter to his boss, Dr Robert Franks, the acting chairman of the paediatrics department. Robotham found a willing ally in Dr Franks, unlike most of those around him, and

Franks ordered him to proceed with the investigation.

Being a cautious man by nature, Dr Robotham proceeded slowly with his inquiries. Although the facts now seemed to point squarely in Genene's direction, he knew there were a number of things which had to be taken into consideration. There was, for instance, the use of heparin, which was being used as an anti-coagulant, sometimes with dire results when someone had given a child too much of it. It was even possible that the drug company who had made it had supplied the wrong dosage. All the possibilities had to be examined.

In the meantime, Genene's behaviour now became quite weird, with her issuing orders left and right to the charge hands, until she gave the impression that she was running the whole show, something that Pat Belko did not take to kindly when she was informed of what was happening.

Though deaths were still going on, the management did not respond with any attempt to put an end to matters, even though the number of fatalities was assuming major proportions. In desperation, Dr Franks had taken his problem to B. H. Corum, the executive director.

Lieutenant Colonel Buford Hubert Corum Jr, to give him his full title, was a man with a great deal of experience, and he arrived at Bexar County Hospital determined to stamp out whatever malpractice might exist between the hospital's four walls. In many respects he was just the sort of man the hospital needed.

He handled the staff severely and ruled over them with a rod of iron, and there is no doubt that he shook the building up and did much to get rid of many of the staff's slapdash methods. But in the one area where he was most needed,

Corum let the hospital down. After examining the possibility that one of the nursing staff might be killing off some of their patients, he decided that the directors had been over-reacting and that no further action on his part was needed.

In the meantime, Jim Robotham had gone back to his files, and what he found in them worried him greatly. There was a series of events which had happened which just should not have happened.

In most cases when a death had occurred, an overdose of heparin seemed to have been the cause of death.

For Patricia Alberti, a thirty-nine-year-old medic on the night shift, there was no doubt in her mind that Genene was killing off her kids. A tall, boot-faced woman with an abrupt manner, she had no hesitation in voicing her convictions. She spoke feelingly of one of the patients most recently in her care. 'I struggled with her for eight hours, and the kid was still alive. The day shift came in and the kid was still alive when they had finished. Genene came in for three hours and the kid was dead.'

To Patricia Alberti it was like having to sit watching a Greek tragedy unfold before her eyes, and in the end she went to her psychiatrist and reported that a nurse had killed off one of her charges, and that absolutely nothing was being done about it. To make matters worse, Patricia Alberti then came on shift just in time to hear Genene give a boy's parents a report on their child who had just been brought in after having been rescued from a fire. 'I'm afraid he would be better off dead,' she told them. 'If he did survive, the child would suffer from brain damage and would have to be institutionalised.' We do not know

58

what the parents' response was, but within a few hours the boy was dead, after having suffered two massive heart attacks. Once again, one suspects that the child was given an overdose of heparin.

The staff nurses then learned that Robotham would be away for a month, and Genene took the opportunity of telling all of them that he had been sent off as he was suffering from a nervous breakdown.

December came and the staff of Bexar County Hospital began to look forward to Christmas. It had been a bad year so far. The previous month had been calm enough, but since then no fewer than seven children had died. Now a young child named Rolando Santos was dying, this time from a simple case of pneumonia which the hospital should have had no trouble in curing.

A Dr Kenneth Copeland had been called in as he was something of an expert in his field, but even he was disturbed by the way the disease was progressing. It was not until the beginning of January that the patient had recovered enough for the doctor to feel that his charge was in the clear. Then, on the afternoon of 9 January, his patient had begun to bleed and he fell into a coma. They knew there were in danger of losing him.

Incredibly, Rolando Santos' condition improved dramatically and five days later he was well enough to go home, mainly due to the efforts of Dr Copeland, who had been determined that the boy should not be left alone whatever the circumstances.

Thanks to the case of Rolando Santos, Jim Robotham had managed to accumulate enough evidence to prove that the patient had been given an overdose of heparin.

Although no one had seen Genene inject the blood thinner, Robotham now felt certain that she *had* injected it.

Although he now had enough evidence to launch an attack on Genene, Franks was hesitant about taxing her with her crimes, arguing that to an outsider they might seem nothing more than the histrionics of an overwrought doctor. Faced with the option of going it alone and running the risk of coming out directly against Franks, Robotham decided to let the matter drop rather than jeopardise his career over something where he could see he would get no support.

One of the amazing things about the case of Genene Jones is how she still managed to get away with it, thanks mainly to the craven-hearted administration who refused to accept facts that were staring them in the face.

And so it had gone on to the bitter end. In the case of young Patrick Zavala, who, after recovering completely from open-heart surgery suddenly died of a heart attack, Genene was seen to grab a syringe and, like a priest sprinkling holy water on his forehead, had made the sign of the cross over him. The sudden death of Patrick Zavala had taken most of the nurses unawares, but they had been more than perturbed over Genene's ritualistic behaviour with the hypodermic needle. But even this was allowed to pass without comment beyond raised eyebrows among themselves.

On 25 January a group of highly placed executives gathered in the executive director's office at the Medical Center Hospital. Among them were B. H. Corum, Bob Franks and Jim Robotham, who had all assembled to discuss what should be done about Genene Jones.

Speaking from his page of scribbled notes, Robotham briefed them, telling them of his suspicions. Speaking of her emotional instability, her hysterical outbursts and her history of illnesses, most of which had been quite imaginary, he then gave them an exhaustive list of disasters which had occurred while she had been there. Then came the question of what they were to do about her. Picking their way through the evidence, which they all knew was the sort of mess that could lead to lawsuits, the assembled group decided to call in the hospital malpractice lawyer, a well-known San Antonio man, who turned out be even more cautious than they were. His name was Paul Green and the only advice he could offer them was that without hard evidence they should proceed only with extreme caution, otherwise they would undoubtedly end up with legal proceedings on their hands. With those words ringing in their ears, the meeting broke up in disorder.

The next step was to call in Dr Alan Conn who arrived in San Antonio late in January 1982. He had come to them with the highest of reputations, thanks to having been on the staff of the Toronto Hospital for Sick Children, probably one of the world's foremost paediatric institutions.

Conn had a six-month sabbatical and decided to spend that time at the San Antonio hospital, where he was to do research on drowning victims. Robotham had been one of his students, and knowing that Conn was coming to San Antonio, Robotham had put his name forward as being the ideal person to investigate everything that had been happening over the last few months in the Intensive Care Unit. His arrival on the scene had annoyed a number of people, including Genene herself who resented investigations being made into the deaths. She had been quite prepared to resign but later withdrew her resignation as it was alien to her nature to quit without a fight.

Before he had even entered the hospital Alan Conn had already dismissed the idea of blaming a nurse for the killing of the children. He had previously had a not dissimilar situation occur at his own hospital and it had led to a lot of unnecessary distress among the staff, thanks mainly to the fact that a nurse had allegedly killed off a number of young patients. It had led to wholesale dismissal of members of staff, and the reputation of the hospital had suffered. He had no intention of contributing to the same sort of thing happening at San Antonio.

All that resulted from Conn's present investigation was that he put in a report stating that Robotham and Belko had failed to provide the sort of leadership needed. Apart from also attacking a number of nurses for sloppy work, the report ended with the recommendation that Robotham and Belko should be dismissed – the only two people who had made an effort to find the murderer.

It is hard to match this appalling and long series of misadventures which had gone on. Genene emerged smelling of roses. In due course the following testimonial appeared in her file:

TO WHOM IT MAY CONCERN
Due to the recommendation of a recent Pediatric Intensive Care Site Team Visit, the Pediatric ICU is being converted to an all RN staff composition at Medical Center Hospital.

Mrs Genene Jones has been employed in the Pediatric ICU since 1978. This move in no way reflects on her performance in the unit. She has gained valuable knowledge and experience in pediatric care nursing. During her time of employment this employee has been loyal, dependable and trustworthy.

Mrs Genene Jones LVN has been an asset to the Bexar County Hospital District, and I would recommend continued employment.

It was signed by Pat Belko and composed with the assistance of Virginia Mousseau.

In the March of the same year Genene Jones did resign from the Medical Center Hospital. She told her mother that she had become tired of having to deal with so many inefficient doctors who were often not aware of what they were doing. Her mother knew her well enough not to question this statement and let the matter pass without comment. Besides, her daughter was showing visible signs of strain and obviously needed a rest.

Genene's resignation did not mean she had retired permanently from her profession. Far from it! She took a number of jobs in local hospitals and then accepted a job with the Santa Rosa Medical Center in downtown San Antonio. Most of her time there she spent idling away the hours in some quiet spot in the hospital while she went through cigarette after cigarette. Suddenly, on 22 July she announced that she would not do another day's work, and true to her word, she stalked out of the building, never to return.

When we next hear of her she had found herself a three-bedroomed house in Kerrville, a suburb of San Antonio, where her landlady was Kathleen Holland, who had bought the house as an investment and had then let it out to Genene, who had moved into it happily with her two children.

From the beginning the two women seemed to get on well together. Kathy Holland, for her part, had only the greatest respect for Genene, whom she considered had been a victim of male chauvinism throughout her working life, and for whose medical abilities she had nothing but admiration. On the other side of the coin, Genene was genuinely grateful to Kathy Holland for providing such pleasant accommodation in which she could bring up her children.

There is no doubt that Kathy Holland had only got where she was with the greatest of difficulty. Born in 1946, the daughter of two factory workers, she had been a bookish child who had grown up the hard way, her mother and father being two people who liked to spend their money on drink, which they consumed in large quantities when they were not fighting with each other.

Kathleen had to abandon her schooling at an early age when her father suddenly died of pneumonia. She took a job in a pizza parlour in order to support her mother, but the law required her to return to school where she behaved so atrociously that the principal had refused to let her continue her education.

It was soon after that she married a librarian named Larry Doyle, who was some twelve years her senior. With him behind her, she eventually got a job at Cornell

University in New York. With Doyle continually at her elbow and driving her hard all the way, she had gone on to take her bachelor's degree, majoring in anatomy and physiology.

It was not until she was aged thirty and doing some work at the Bexar County Hospital that she finally decided to specialise in paediatrics. She and her husband then settled in an area close to San Antonio. But by then she was already tired of her husband's demanding ways, and by mutual agreement the couple had filed for divorce which went through in the July of that year.

Free of the tyranny, it was like starting a new life with no one driving her on all the time. She was free at last to do what she wanted to do, and for a while she lived with a retired air force colonel whom she later married. She then opened a small medical centre of her own which had three examination rooms plus a private office for herself, and a number of smaller rooms which could be used for other purposes.

She now had a promising career in front of her, and furthermore also had a number of friends she could rely on. These, of course, included her husband and Genene Jones, who had already made it quite clear that her services were available.

After their marriage, Kathy and her husband spent the next few months living in makeshift accommodation while their property was being got ready for occupation.

By the time Kathy Holland had started her clinic, she had gathered around her a number of thoroughly unsuitable people. There was Gwen Grantner, a thirty-three-year-old woman whom she had taken on as a secretary-receptionist and who spoke with a strong cockney accent, even though she had never been to England in her life. There was also Catherine Ferguson, an oddball eccentric whom Genene had employed to take care of her two children only to discover that she had spent some time in a Texan mental institution, and of course, there was Genene herself who was just raring to go, as well she might after being absent from the medical profession for so long.

Just before the new clinic was launched, Kathy ran into Robotham. 'I hear you're getting into business with Genene? If that's the case, I think you should think twice about it,' and he went on to tell her something of his suspicions. However, when it came down to hard facts, Kathy thought him vague and she went home unconvinced.

The opening of the clinic proved to be something of an anticlimax as they had only one patient in all day. But Kathy Holland was not unduly worried as she knew that it took time to establish a business, and after all, it was only the first day they had opened their doors.

Although nothing of significance had happened on that first day, Kathy was glad to get home to her husband. He had spent countless hours at the site of their new home and they had met only when they were both reeling with tiredness.

They had both been looking forward to the weekend but before it came round a child was brought in suffering from a staphyloccal infection. Kathy not being there at the time, Genene began examining the child herself. The child's blood sugar level was dangerously low, and she knew that if they didn't act fast he would soon lapse into a coma. She did the only practical thing and telephoned for an ambulance.

Within minutes the sick child was on its way to hospital. As it turned out she had done the only sensible thing possible. Within a week the child had been cured and Kathy Holland's reputation had soared, although it had really been Genene's prompt action which had saved the child.

Over the course of the next few months Kathy Holland's practice went from strength to strength. There were, inevitably, some deaths among the young patients, but they had happened under normal circumstances. Was it possible that Genene's abnormal condition had burnt itself out, and that from now on she would give no cause for concern? Certainly in the months that followed Genene behaved in a normal, responsible manner towards her patients.

Suddenly, in the middle of September they found themselves having to deal with an influx of emergencies. Roughly coinciding with this was also a sudden rush of ugly rumours, first about Kathy Holland, who it was claimed was a lesbian, with nothing to back up the claim other than the fact that she wore mannish clothes and cut her hair short. No sooner had these rumours begun to die down than a fresh spate of gossip began, this time concerning Genene, who was said to be a baby killer. Genene heard the rumours that were flying around Kerrville, and she responded by taking an overdose – certainly not enough to kill her, but a carefully calculated amount that would be enough to necessitate her having her stomach pumped before she was released from hospital, seemingly as good as new. The suicide bid had been for dramatic effect only, but it did the trick. The critics were silenced and Genene was allowed to get on with her life.

But the matter did not completely end there. News of the

rumours had reached the ears of the Texas Rangers, who began making inquiries of their own. Heading them was a man named Joe Davis who was very much a member of the old school who doggedly pursued a criminal until he was brought to justice. When Genene was released from hospital after her overdose, Joe Davis was waiting to see her. He asked if he might interview her, and she readily agreed.

The same day he took her to have a polygraph examination. He knew such a test did not carry any weight in a court of law, but it was a useful investigative tool which was liable to throw some people off balance when they undertook it.

In his questioning, Davis had taxed Genene with the murders, which she had stoutly denied committing. According to the graph from the truth machine, Genene had lied. If the machine was to be believed, Genene's responses to what had been put to her had all been lies. Her only answer to Joe Davis' accusation that she had lied to every question he asked was that as far as she was concerned, she had been telling the truth.

The next day Joe Davis took Kathy Holland for a lie-detector test. According to the report printed out after the test, Kathy had lied no fewer than four times. As we know, all that Kathy had been guilty of was nothing except to be over-protective towards Genene. Even so, she began to realise that she was putting herself at risk and so she told Genene that it would no longer be expedient to have her around the place. As for the polygraph, John Maxwell, who had conducted the examination, sheepishly informed her that she had failed the test because 'she was feeling a lot of guilt because she had taken a nurse on her staff, knowing she was a prime suspect in San Antonio over a similar incident'.

Without a job again now, and without Kathy Holland behind her, Genene moved out of the house she had been renting from her and took another house in San Angelo, a West Texas city where she hoped she would disappear into oblivion.

Knowing that he was going to get nowhere with his polygraph test in a court of law, Davis decided to approach Ron Sutton who was a District Attorney and was between cases, having just experienced a heavy defeat in a triple murder case. Only the most superficial examination of what facts were available was enough to convince Sutton of the complexity of the case and he began to wonder if he was taking on too much. The one thing he didn't want was to lose two cases in a row.

Nevertheless he decided to take it on, knowing that it would attract a great deal of public attention. A vain man, he saw himself catching the headlines with a display of legal histrionics that would match those of Perry Mason, one of his favourite TV characters.

In fact it was not until 13 May of the following year that Genene was finally charged with the murder of some of her patients. As all the charges carried a maximum sentence of ninety years, it seemed as if for the first time she really had something to worry about.

In all, the grand jury issued eight criminal charges against her, and as she had not appeared in court to hear them read out to her, she was now a wanted criminal.

Only hours later the Texas Rangers tracked her down to

a home in Odessa, from where she was planning to leave the next morning in the company of a nineteen-year-old male nurse named Garron Turk, whom she had secretly married. She had decided that she would marry him and then disappear into the anonymity of Colorado. Placing her under arrest, the Rangers quickly put her under lock and key in the local jail.

For the trial, the judge had appointed Bill Chenault as her defence lawyer, and then perhaps realising that he was a fledgling in criminal law, had given her Joe Grady Tuck, a former DA now working in private practice, and considered to be one of the best defence lawyers around.

There were two preliminary hearings before the trial proper began, in January 1984, and in the first of them Sutton suggested that the only reason she had married her new husband was because she saw him as a good excuse for disappearing to Colorado.

'That is not true,' Genene Jones said coolly. 'We only discussed it as a possibility.'

Sutton produced so many witnesses as to make Genene's chances of surviving the trial slim. One of them was Kathy Holland, who spoke against her at considerable length, though long before this the judge had decided to move the trial to the Williamson County Courthouse in Georgia. In all, the prosecution called forty-four witnesses. The defence counsel could only summon up seven witnesses before they had to rest their case. Now that all the evidence for and against Genene had been presented, it was up to the judge and jury to decide her fate.

Just how sane was Genene Jones when she committed her terrible crimes? In many people's minds that question had already been answered at the beginning of the trial when she had undergone a series of tests which proved that she was completely sane. But it was not as clear cut as that. In all, it is thought that she killed sixteen children. Had she reached a state of mental instability where she saw herself as a Godlike figure who had the right to decide when it was time for certain of her charges to be killed? Who can tell? All we know for certain is that for a space of time it was she who decided who should live or die. Whatever the truth of it is, she paid for it with a sentence of 159 years.

THE
WIGWAM MURDER

Although not one hundred per cent Red Indian, August Sangret was still enough of one to be immediately recognisable as such, with his swarthy skin, hook nose, lank black hair and a pair of smouldering black eyes that looked out on the world with a burning intensity; tell-tale clues that betrayed the fact that he had Red Indian blood running through his veins.

Actually he was a French Canadian who had been brought up in Saskatchewan, where he had rapidly acquired a record for being a hard man with a long history of robbery with violence. For all that, he had an air of animal magnetism, and it was undoubtedly that which had attracted him to Pearl Wolfe, a blonde girl who sported an Eton crop, and who had been strictly brought up by nuns until she rebelled against them and had run away from the convent, often sleeping rough when she could not afford a room for the night.

Among her many pick-ups was Sangret, and for some time they made their abode in a disused cricket pavilion near Godalming, where he was stationed with the army, until they were caught by an air-raid warden who moved them on. It was then that Sangret built her a series of weather-proof constructions in the manner of an Indian-style wigwam. Made mostly from bracken and heather which grew plentifully on Hankley Common where Sangret had put up his makeshift hovels, they provided little more than a shelter for their love-making, but they were still better than nothing.

For a while the affair thrived until Pearl Wolfe became pregnant by Sangret, who now found himself under pressure to marry her. He assured her that he would do so, and as a measure of his good faith he showed her an official form that he got from his CO, allowing him to marry her. All that it now needed was his signature at the bottom of the form. According to the evidence, it seemed that Sangret fully intended to marry Pearl Wolfe. This made her very happy. According to the nuns who brought her up she had been committing a mortal sin, and by regularising the union she would once more be admitted to the church. Although she would have been the last person to admit it, she secretly welcomed the idea of having the comfort and security of the Catholic church behind her.

When she abruptly disappeared from public view somewhere towards the middle of September 1942 there were very few of her friends who did not know about the affair she had been having with Sangret, of whom she had always spoken highly. The couple had also been seen together around Godalming when they tried to find a room for her to go to when she had the baby.

When Inspector Webb was called in to find out what had happened to her, the first person to help him with his inquiries was August Sangret, who freely admitted to having an affair with her before she had so mysteriously disappeared.

For some time nothing happened, until one day two young marines out on an exercise saw a girl's arm sticking up out of the ground. They immediately reported it to the officer in charge of the exercise who then notified the local police, who brought in the noted pathologist, Keith Simpson.

Even the briefest of examinations was enough to tell them that she had been brutally murdered. The body was already in an advanced state of putrefaction and was crawling with maggots, which made their task extremely distasteful, but even at this stage they were able to tell that the girl had been bludgeoned about the head as well as being stabbed several times. Simpson was then allowed to remove the body to his London mortuary, where the maggots were killed off in a bath of carbolic acid.

With the body now in a more approachable state for examination, he set about restoring the skeleton where possible, mainly wiring together the smashed pieces of the girl's skull, from which he was able to conclude the sort of weapon which had killed her – a long, heavy stick.

Sangret's undoing was the discovery of her handbag on the common, containing a rosary, a Roman Catholic pamphlet and an unfinished letter to Sangret, saying once again that she was pregnant, and reminding him of his promise to marry her.

The police, led by Inspector Greeno, who had been allocated to the case by Scotland Yard, knew from that letter that in all probability Sangret was the murderer. All they needed now was the murder weapon. They did not have to look far; one of the policemen assigned to searching the area near to where the body had been found, discovered a yard-long heavy stake with some blonde hairs still adhering to it.

Around Christmas, when the police were still deciding whether or not to arrest Sangret, another piece of evidence turned up. This was the 'permission to marry' form issued to Sangret, and was found by Inspector Greeno lying in a crumpled ball near the wigwam on the common. It was still unsigned, and proved to him that Sangret had already decided that he was not going to marry the dead girl, after all. In the meantime Sangret had been circulating a lot of cock and bull stories about Pearl Wolfe's disappearance which were all such a farrago of nonsense that Inspector Greeno dismissed them out of hand.

It was about then that Greeno decided the time had come for him to get from Sangret a long, detailed account of his movements and to get him to sign a statement.

He left Sangret kicking his heels in the guard room before he made his appearance. When he did arrive he wasted no time in coming to the point. 'I want you to tell me all you can about your association with Miss Wolfe,' he said, sitting himself down in front of Sangret.

'Of course,' said Sangret politely. 'But first I must ask permission to go to the washroom.'

Greeno reluctantly allowed him to go while he waited impatiently for him to return. When he did come back, Sangret listened impassively to the barrage of questions that were thrown at him. One of them concerned his army knife which had been issued so that he could cut up his bread and open tins of meat with it. It was at this point that Greeno formally cautioned him.

'Of course, she might have killed herself,' Sangret said hopefully.

He then made a long, rambling statement amounting to some 17,000 words. Far from incriminating himself with some incautious remark, he managed to walk away from the interview a free man, there still not being enough evidence against him to bring about his conviction.

After Sangret had left him, Greeno sat there quietly, wondering just how they were going to be able to convict him the way things were going. As so often happens with a murder case, a rare piece of luck came his way when one of the soldiers at the camp reported that a knife like the one that Greeno was looking for had been found in the waste pipe in one of the washrooms. Greeno remembered at once that Sangret had left him to go to the washroom; and he knew that it had to be the missing knife.

Sangret was arrested and charged with the murder of Pearl Wolfe, only five months after her murder.

Before the trial Greeno showed Sangret the knife he had found and taxed Sangret with the murder. Although he identified the knife as belonging to him he still denied any knowledge of the murder. 'Pearl used to carry it in her handbag,' he said. 'She told me she had got it from the soldier she had gone out with before me. That knife was never given back to Pearl after she lent it to someone.'

'Would you recognise it?' Greeno asked.

'I'm not sure,' Sangret faltered.

At the trial it was suggested that Sangret had buried her on high ground because he had reverted to his Indian origins. All the writers who have covered this case have given this piece of evidence as being proof that Sangret was guilty. This, of course, is nonsense, as no man in a highly disturbed state of mind such as his when he murdered Pearl, would have been bothered with such niceties as trying to observe ancient Red Indian burial customs.

At the trial, the knife was presented as a key piece of evidence, which indeed it was, and Sangret undoubtedly hanged himself when he hid it in the washroom drain. He could only have known the nature of her injuries if he had inflicted them on her himself. Otherwise, why bother to hide the knife? It had a distinctive design to the blade, and was obviously the one used to stab Pearl Wolfe.

Sangret stuck to his story to the last, though he admitted that he and Pearl had quarrelled on the day of the murder. 'But I never did kill her,' he said.

'This is a lie,' Mr Eric Neve, acting for the prosecution, told him. 'I suggest to you that this girl who was telling you that she was going to have a baby was becoming a bit of a nuisance and you were prepared to shake her off any way you could.'

'What for?' asked Sangret, who seemed determined to argue against everything, however much the evidence stood against him.

'So that you might be free to carry on with another woman in Glasgow, or anywhere else, for that matter,' Mr Neve said brutally.

Sangret sat throughout the trial without any visible sign of emotion. After hearing all the evidence the jury went out and spent two hours deliberating on their verdict. They found him guilty, but added the rider that a strong recommendation for mercy should be considered. Their recommendation was ignored and the judge gave him the death sentence which was carried out at Wandsworth Prison on 29 April 1943. Before being executed he confessed to the crime.

THE
SINGING MURDERER

He was a pleasant-faced young GI who was always smiling and willing to exchange pleasantries with anyone who would give him the time of day. He also laughed easily – perhaps too easily for some people, who found that there was something not quite right about him. For one thing, he seemed unstable, and there was also something odd about the manner in which he could suddenly stop and listen, as if enchanted, to someone singing. When asked why, he said he was fascinated with the voice of the singer, which invariably belonged to a young woman. He said he liked young people with soft voices. What he did not bother to add on those occasions was that he would like to capture their voices.

The year was 1942 and he was stationed in Melbourne at the time, and to those Australians he met in the bars he was fond of frequenting, he was a well-known figure. They knew him as 'The Mad Yank' because of his strange obsession with beautiful voices, and particularly those belonging to attractive young women.

What the people of Melbourne did not know was that in Edward Leonski they were harbouring a human time bomb. His parents had both been mad and had spent part of their existence in a lunatic asylum, and the son was also insane, and within a month of arriving in Australia had become a homicidal killer. The fact that he had survived for so long without being put away is a sore reflection on the psychiatrists who handled his case.

The long fugue of death began on 2 May 1942, when Leonski calmly went out one evening and strangled Ivy McLeod as she was on her way home from work. When this was followed a week later by the murder of Pauline Thompson, the police knew they had a serial killer on their hands. After he claimed a third victim, named Gladys Hosking, whose strangled body was discovered lying in the street, they really began to panic because by this time they knew they were dealing with seemingly motiveless murders which made their task almost an impossibility unless they actually caught the killer in the act.

The police had nothing to go on except that Melbourne was full of uniformed troops from all points of the compass, and they felt it was probable that it would be one of these men.

It was then that Leonski gave them a chance of cracking the case. This time the girl he picked up was a young saleswoman named Kathleen Elliott, who looked to him to be a likely victim.

'I was walking along Wimble Street on my way to my home in Park Street,' she recalled afterwards. 'Suddenly I was accosted by an American soldier wearing a fatigue uniform. He asked me if I could spare him a cigarette as they were only allowed ten a day.'

She had abruptly told him she had none.

He then asked if he could walk beside her.

'I suppose I can't stop you,' Miss Elliott had then said in an icy voice which she had hoped would discourage him.

When they had reached her front door and she had placed her key in the lock, the soldier leered at her. 'Aren't you going to invite me in?'

'I can't,' she said to him. 'My husband is in.'

That remark was a downright lie and she had only said it to discourage the soldier. Already she was getting warning signals about him, and those were fully justified for he suddenly grabbed her by the throat. Screaming, she broke free of him and fled along Park Street.

He made no attempt to follow her. Instead, he ambled over to a constable and coolly cadged a cigarette from him before making his way back to his barracks.

Before he reached the camp, where he calmly turned in for the night, he tried to assault another young woman who screamed as Leonski attacked her, and for the second time that night, he was forced to flee.

In the past Melbourne had had the reputation of being one of the most moral towns in Australia. Conservative to the last man, they prided themselves on being a highly respectable unit of society which had the lowest crime rate around. Inevitably, all this changed when Australia went to war. Gambling joints and whorehouses had sprung up to cater to the armed forces of all nations that were now entering the city in droves, bringing a new era of violence and lawlessness. Being unused to dealing with violence on this scale, the police were completely unable to cope with it all and Leonski was able to pursue his murderous career more easily than he would have done in peacetime Melbourne.

Leonski never disclosed when he made his first attack on a woman in Australia. A Mrs Doreen Justice was undoubtedly one of his first victims. A married woman of twenty-two with a baby, she had come to Melbourne from Sydney, after having been advised by her doctor to go there for her health. She had eventually taken a flat in the city and was settling in nicely when one day there was a ring on the front doorbell. She opened it, and a soldier brushed past her. He then pulled her in. 'Take it easy, baby,' he said. 'Don't scream and everything will be all right. If you do scream I will choke you. I like your line. I have taken a fancy to you.'

For someone in such a situation, Mrs Justice had managed to keep cool.

'Whatever are you doing here?' she asked angrily. 'Get out of here!'

The man merely grinned. 'If you don't like my looks, maybe this will tempt you,' he said, pulling a wad of money from his pocket.

'I am not that sort of woman,' Mrs Justice said. 'Now get out of here.'

'That's what you think,' the man said. Up to then he had been smiling all the time. Now he assumed a menacing expression. Suddenly, without warning he had grabbed her by the throat and squeezed it so violently that Mrs Justice was aware that her tongue was sticking out of her mouth.

He then picked her up from the floor where she had fallen, and carried her into the bedroom, where he flung her on the bed. She struggled with him for a few seconds and then cried out.

'Water,' she managed to croak. 'I must have some water.'

He growled, 'You are trying to trick me.' But despite this he allowed her to get up from the bed and he then led her to the kitchen, where she drew a glass of water from the tap.

She had barely finished drinking when she heard someone coming down the passageway outside the front door. She managed to open the door partly and cried out, 'For God's sake help me!' After a brief struggle, she fled down the passageway, where her neighbour, Mrs O'Neill was just returning to her flat next door.

'Help me,' she managed to gasp out. 'Please help me.'

Mrs O'Neill was about to answer her when she saw Leonski lurking in the doorway. She immediately called to her brother-in-law who had been accompanying her home. It was at this point that Leonski made a run for it, disappearing down the stairs before the brother-in-law could come to the rescue.

The experience had been a terrifying one for Mrs Justice – and one that she was not likely to forget in a hurry, but fortunately she suffered no ill effects, except that her throat was sore for several days afterwards.

Despite the scare that Leonski had given her, Mrs Justice stayed on in the flat until the end of the month, when she returned to Sydney where she spent several months regaling people with her near miraculous escape. Leonski had been quite unperturbed by having been almost caught and was already planning new forays in night-time Melbourne.

When he did strike again only a few days later, he politely accosted a woman a few years older than himself and asked her to go skating with him. The woman refused, and, unbeknown to her, he shadowed her to her home in South Melbourne. Only yards away from where she lived he closed in on her, and grabbing her by the throat, he whispered, 'I'm going to kill a girl tonight. You might as well be the one.'

Although petrified with fear she managed to scream before Leonski's hands tightened around her throat. Fortunately a man heard her and came running and Leonski ran off into the night.

In the same month there followed the murder of Ivy McLeod on 2 May when her strangled body was found in the doorway of a shop. We know that Leonski was responsible for her murder because when he was later caught, he brazenly admitted the fact, mentioning in the process that he had nearly been caught murdering her by a group of drunken soldiers with whom he had been drinking earlier in the evening at the nearby Bleak House hotel.

Until they were faced with the ugly realities of the death of Ivy McLeod and the others that had followed almost immediately afterwards, the police had made no real effort to capture Leonski. Not that they had a lot to go on: a glimpse of a soldier who might or might not be the man they were looking for, and a check on some 1,700 American paybooks, from which nothing had resulted which represented anything concrete that might lead them to the killer.

There was no doubt that a mammoth task lay before the police in a city that was positively crawling with uniformed soldiery. They dutifully screened every hotel and bar in the whole city, asking questions and striking up conversations with complete strangers in the hope that someone might give them a clue to the identity of the murderer. All to no avail. That is until four detectives strolled into the bar of the Royal Park Hotel, North Melbourne. All of them ordered a beer, and when it arrived they sipped at it slowly while they gazed around at the other bar occupants. 'Watch that Yank over there. Look, he's grinning at us now, the ape.'

The detective sitting next to the speaker shrugged and buried his face in his beer. 'You could be right,' he said. 'I wonder if he knows we're police officers. He certainly looks as if he's got strong-looking hands. It might be worth a check.'

'Let's ask at the station nearby to see the constable who suggested we take a look around this area. You know the one. The one who was approached by a soldier, asking him for a cigarette.'

'I'll step around to the station and see if I can find him,' one of the detectives said, slipping from his chair.

He had no sooner left than the soldier also downed his drink and left, with the other detectives hastily following in his wake. Their friend who had gone off in search of the constable must have been extremely lucky, for he was able to return with him within a couple of minutes.

'Well, is that him?' he asked. 'Is that the man you saw that night when he tried to cadge a cigarette from you?'

It is unfortunate that the constable's memory should have failed him on this occasion. If he had remembered the killer's face there is no doubt that Gladys Hosking would not have died and her body been discovered near the military camp grounds close to Royal Park.

The constable shook his head. 'I'm sorry, but that's not the man you're looking for. I've never seen him before in my life.'

We move on to 20 May, by which time the police had a clearer idea of whom they were looking for, having had a good description of him from Mrs Justice, and heard reports coming in of a baby-faced Yank who had sounded as if he might fit the bill very well.

On that day thousands of troops had been milling around the city, and, having been alerted to this fact, they were hoping to catch a glimpse of someone answering to his description. It had been raining all day, as was normal in Melbourne at that time of the year, with the rain coming down in sheets, and they were about to return to camp in a thoroughly dispirited frame of mind, when a soldier excitedly caught the sleeve of Detective Ernest Craig, who had gone out with them on their search.

'That's him! The man they call the baby-faced Yank! I'd recognise him anywhere.'

Almost before he had gone another half dozen paces, the baby-faced Yank, more formally known as Edward Leonski, found himself facing an array of menacing weapons.

The next day he was given a vigorous grilling by the police, and blandly confessed to all the murders. At no point did he show the slightest remorse, or seem to think he had done anything wrong. In due course he was officially arrested, subsequently court-martialled and brought to trial, where he was found guilty and sentenced to death. In

Neville Heath is driven away from court having been charged with the murders of Margery Gardener and Doreen Marshall. (*Press Association*)

Police officers examine the soil in Branksome Chine where the body of Doreen Marshall was found. (*Popperfoto*)

The announcement on the gates at Pentonville Prison that Neville Heath had been hanged on 16 October 1946. (*Popperfoto*)

Sergeant Mick Emmett-Dunne and his new wife Maria, the widow of Reginald 'Tich' Watters. (*Associated Press*)

Genene Ann Jones shown in 1984 after she had been convicted of the murder of one infant, though it was thought that she had killed as many as sixteen children in her care. (*Associated Press*)

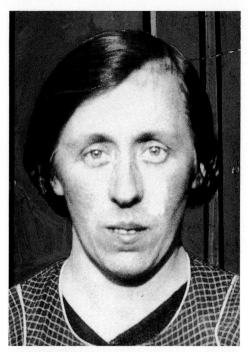

Left: Dorothea Waddingham, who poisoned two residents at her nursing home. (*Popperfoto*)

Below: A huge crowd gathered outside the court as Nurse Waddingham was found guilty of murder. (*Popperfoto*)

these more enlightened times, more consideration would have been given to the fact that he was clearly raving mad, and there was a history of insanity in the family, but these facts were ignored by the judge and jury, and he was sentenced to death by hanging.

In the last weeks leading up to his execution he turned into something of a health freak, never failing to take his morning exercise by walking up and down the long flagged corridors of the prison, as well as turning handsprings and even indulging in executing catherine wheels before his incredulous jailors. One way and another he evinced a great deal of faith in keeping himself in a state of physical fitness, though one would have thought it was a little late in the day for him to be concerned about his health.

He also played softball for hours against the wall of his prison cell, and spent the rest of his time reading a biography of the infamous Ned Kelly. It was as if there was a part of him that refused to face up to the reality that his days on earth were numbered.

His execution took place on 9 November 1942, and he was hanged in the old Melbourne Jail where his hero, Ned Kelly, had met his end. Immediately prior to his being hanged, right up to the point where he was led out to his execution, he sang, thereby earning himself the nickname 'the singing murderer' which was bestowed upon him by certain members of the press.

THE
LETHAL NURSE

Dorothea Waddingham was a plain woman, almost painfully so to anyone meeting her for the first time. A lank-haired, lantern-jawed female with black, bulging eyes, she was not the sort of person to whom you would feel like entrusting your life, although she used to refer to herself as The Angel of Mercy, being a nurse, albeit an unqualified one. What is even more surprising is that she managed to catch herself a husband, and in the course of time had also acquired a lover named Ronald Joseph Sullivan, who, by all accounts, seems to have been an amiable jug-eared man with a pleasant manner. The last man, in fact, you would have expected to land himself with Dorothea Waddingham, who turned out to be directly responsible for him going on trial for murder. He was saved from the gallows only by the intervention of Justice Rayner Goddard, who directed the jury to find him not guilty through lack of evidence.

For the beginning of this sorry saga of greed and murder, we must go back to Dorothea Waddingham's early life, which seems to have been one of perpetual petty crime. Originally from Hucknall, near Nottingham, she began her working life as a factory hand and then went up the social scale a fraction by becoming a ward orderly at the Burton-on-Trent Workhouse Infirmary. It was while she was there that she met and married Thomas Leech, an already sick man. His health was so poor, in fact, that he only worked for three months in all the time they were together.

Why she married him remains something of a mystery, as it must have been obvious from the start that he was going to be a dead loss as a provider. But she seems to have looked after him well enough in the nine years they were married, before he finally succumbed to cancer of the throat.

During that time, however, she had taken herself a lover, the thirty-nine-year-old Ronald Sullivan. Once they had decently buried her husband, the two of them decided to set up a nursing home for the care of the sick and elderly in Devon Drive, Nottingham.

To begin with the venture seems to have been a highly lucrative one, especially as they had received accreditation from the County Nursing Association, who put people their way.

It was from the County Nursing Association in 1935 that they received two patients, the almost ninety-year-old Mrs Baguley and her fifty-year-old daughter, Ada, who was suffering from creeping paralysis, which meant she was in an even worse state than her mother. They both needed constant care and attention, and were indeed determined to get it, often driving Nurse Waddingham and Sullivan to distraction with their frequent demands, which were not always strictly necessary.

Even allowing for the fact that the Baguleys knew they were nearing the end of their lives, and could therefore be forgiven for their often cantankerous behaviour, it must have been very wearing to look after them.

Not surprisingly, it all began to get Nurse Waddingham down. For one thing, Ada Baguley had already knocked over a lamp and set light to the furnishings, and there was no telling what she might do next.

To make matters worse, she lost her other resident patient, a Miss Kemp, who had been under treatment from a Doctor Manfield. Her sudden death now left them with a financial hole which could not easily be filled since there were no other patients in the offing. She was now left with only the Baguleys, who were by now so ill that they both had to be dressed even for sitting up in bed all day. On top of all the extra work, Dorothea had the utmost difficulty in making ends meet. Having to feed and support her five children as well as herself and her husband on £6 per week was something that even the most thrifty and ingenious housewife could not hope to achieve.

In May 1935 she went to the Baguleys with a proposition: if Ada Baguley rewrote her will, leaving her estate to Nurse Waddingham, she would undertake to care for them both until the end of their days. Dorothea Waddingham knew she had the whip hand in this instance, for without her and Sullivan to look after them the Baguleys would have been forced to pay for care in the General Hospital, which would have rapidly eaten away their modest savings.

On 6 May of that year Ada Baguley rewrote her will, leaving £1,600 to Nurse Waddingham in exchange for her promise to look after Ada Baguley and her mother until the end of their days. Six days later the mother expired. Her death was put down to old age. With one down and one to go, Nurse Waddingham's life seemed to have taken on a more hopeful aspect.

Ada Baguley died on 11 September 1935. Nurse Waddingham let it be known that in her opinion she had died due to a sudden cerebral haemorrhage, probably brought on by over-indulging herself with a box of chocolates that had been given to her by a friend named Mrs Briggs. There was no post-mortem. This was perhaps hardly surprising as there had been nothing to indicate that foul play might have been responsible for Ada's death.

Immediately following the demise of Ada Baguley, Nurse Waddingham produced a letter purporting to be from her, which stated that she would like her body to be cremated as soon as possible, and that they should not bother to inform any of her surviving relatives. The funeral took place a few days later and was a quiet affair, attended only by a man named Frederick Gilbert, a former fiancé of Ada's of many years ago, who had attended the funeral as a sentimental homage to a love affair that had ended more than twenty years earlier. After the funeral he disappeared from the scene and was never heard of again. Did he learn in the fulness of time that Nurse Waddingham had murdered Ada in order to make life more tolerable for herself and Sullivan, who seems to have played a strange role in the affair?

On the one hand we have the comments of Mr Justice Goddard, who had ordered Sullivan's release through lack of evidence, and on the other, it seems inconceivable that Sullivan could have had no knowledge of what was going on

94

in Nurse Waddingham's mind when she killed the mother and daughter.

Nurse Waddingham's insistence that the cremation should be carried out with all speed aroused the suspicions of Dr Cyril Banks, the Nottingham Medical Officer, who far from acceding to the request for a hasty cremation, instead ordered a post-mortem. Dr Robert Lynch, who carried it out, stated in his report that there was no reason why death should have occurred from a cerebral haemorrhage. What he did find was more than three grains of morphine in the body. As a result of this, Mrs Baguley's remains were also exhumed and sufficient morphine was found in the corpse to prove that she had also been poisoned.

Dorothea Waddingham and Ronald Sullivan were both arrested and charged with their murders.

If it had not been for the fact that she had spent most of her adult life involved in some form of crime or another, one could almost feel sorry for Dorothea Waddingham. She had had a difficult time with the Baguleys, who had run Ronald and her ragged in their attempts to keep them happy for what was a paltry sum even in those days. Nothing can excuse cold-blooded murder, but Nurse Waddingham had suffered more than most before she had decided, in her desperation, to do away with both of the Baguleys. That she did so was more out of sheer necessity for survival at all costs, than for any other reason.

Having been caught out, it was doubly unfortunate that she should have been brought before Justice Rayner Goddard, who was appointed a High Court Judge on the King's Division in 1932. He was a traditionalist and a strong believer in both corporal punishment and the death penalty, and also a staunch believer in retribution being observed. Neither had he any desire to find any mitigating circumstances just because the accused was a woman. To say that he pursued the accused with unholy zest would have been an unfair statement, but in the case of Ronald Sullivan he made a point of seeing that justice was done by asking the jury to dismiss the case for lack of evidence.

At one point in the trial of Dorothea Waddingham, who now stood alone in the dock, it was pointed out by the prosecution that on the day before Ada Baguley's death, Waddingham had fed her two heavy meals, a point which Mr Justice Goddard pounced on with alacrity. 'Can you, as men of common sense,' he asked the jury, 'think that anyone in their right mind would give a woman suffering from sharp abdominal pains that were so bad that morphia had to be given her for three nights, two helpings of roast pork and baked potatoes, followed by two portions of fruit pie?'

Nurse Waddingham was found guilty by the jury and sentenced to be hanged at Winson Green Prison. The sentence was duly carried out on 16 April 1936.

Despite the jury's appeal for mercy, which Mr Justice Goddard ignored when handing out the sentence, her death on the gallows was one more reason why a Royal Commission then sitting decreed that capital punishment should be brought to an end. Mr Justice Goddard had this to say to the Royal Commission: 'I see no reason why a woman convicted of murder should not hang,' he said bluntly.

No doubt he would have been one of the first to vote

against the Homicide Act when it was put forward in March 1957, which put a stop to many of the hangings. From then on executions could only be carried out for five reasons, which did not include murder by poisoning, with the result that Nurse Waddingham would not have hanged.

Even right up to the very last there was a great deal of reluctance to do away with the death penalty, which had made itself evident at the first reading of Sidney Silverman's Bill, asking for the abolition of capital punishment, when it was utterly rejected by the House of Lords, after its defeat by a narrow margin. Even when it was passed, the State was still able to evoke one of the five clauses under which a prisoner could still be hanged. In the next eight and a half years no fewer than thirty-four people were hanged.

THE MURDER
THAT THREATENED
AN EMPIRE

It was the year of 1909 when the golden age of Vienna was drawing to a close, especially in the world of music, which had seen its best period during the nineteenth century when the melodies of Johann Strauss II were being whistled by practically every errand boy in the city. Now there was a new breed of composer around, people like Igor Stravinsky or Claude Debussy, who composed ballet music for Diaghilev's *Ballets Russes* which had already done so much to promote the interest of the public in some of the greatest names in music. But now something had gone from Vienna, leaving it more like any other European city.

All this must have gone right over the heads of the Austrian High Command, who had never been known for its pursuit of the arts. As far as the *Ballets Russes* was concerned, it would be fair to say that the officers who served in the High Command were far more interested in pursuing the ladies of the *corps de ballet*, than in the productions that Diaghilev was putting on.

Probably one of the most ambitious officers in the High Command was Adolph Hofrichter, who had recently been overlooked for promotion. Burning with resentment, he hit on the idea of removing most of the High Command by sending a dozen boxes of pills laced with a fatal dose of cyanide of potassium to each of them. Accompanying each box was the following letter:

These nerve-strengthening pills are guaranteed by the highest medical authorities to be an admirable method of securing their purpose and to be absolutely harmless. Judge for yourself. The box must be opened with care and their contents swallowed with a draught of water. The results will be startling. The pills should be taken soon as exposure to air spoils them. Awaiting your further orders which will be carried out with discretion and rapidity.

This was followed by an address in Vienna and signed Charles Francis. On the surface there was no difference between this letter and any other piece of advertising.

Fortunately, most of the recipients threw both the letter and the pills into their waste bins. There was only one exception, and that was Captain Richard Mader, who was employed in the War Office in Vienna. That evening, while writing to his fiancée, he was sufficiently curious about the pills to take a couple of them. In less than a minute he had dropped down dead.

It was thought that the cause of death was due to a heart attack, and the army would have buried him unquestion- ingly if Captain Mader's relatives had not insisted on having a post-mortem carried out. Their suspicions concerning Captain Mader's sudden death had been aroused when one of his comrades told them that he had happened to mention that he had received some pills from an unknown source. The post-mortem revealed that Captain Mader had died from an overdose of cyanide of potassium. A full inquiry was immediately set afoot, with the Emperor Franz Josef taking an active interest in the proceedings.

A reward of 2,000 kronen was offered to anyone who caught the culprit, and a mixed body of experts, with the chief of police leading them, was put on the case.

'The man who plotted this foul deed must be found,' the Emperor told the chief of police. 'No matter who he is or what he is. Now don't let me see you again until you have found him.'

At first the task seemed to be a hopeless one. The murderer appeared to have covered his tracks with remarkable care. But what worried those seeking to hunt him down was the lack of motive. Captain Mader had been a popular officer without an enemy in the world. Then someone discovered that no fewer than eleven other officers had also received a box of pills, and that all of them had graduated from the Military Academy in 1905. They also learned that a Lieutenant Hofrichter had graduated at the same time and had later been rejected for a permanent General Staff post after holding the position in a temporary capacity. From then on it was only a matter of time before they homed in on him, with the War Ministry issuing a statement to the effect that they suspected Adolph Hofrichter of having carried out the murder, 'with a probability that was almost a certainty'.

Despite all the incriminating evidence with which he was

faced, Hofrichter kept calm and protested that he was innocent. He had a perfectly logical answer to everything. Some boxes they had discovered had been bought merely to contain some of his wife's trinkets, and the capsules had been meant for his dogs.

'And what sort of medicine would that be?' he was asked.

'It's a worm mixture,' he told them.

The capsules were duly analysed and found to be a compound used as a dog medicine. But the committee were still not satisfied, feeling that Hofrichter's explanation was somewhat flimsy. He was then put under close arrest and removed to the military prison in Vienna.

Although it had no relevance to the case, his situation was not helped when a village girl with whom he had had an affair committed suicide, leaving a note condemning Hofrichter for betraying his promise to marry her. To Hofrichter the affair had meant nothing more than a harmless flirtation, especially as he was already married.

In many ways Hofrichter was something of a Jekyll and Hyde character. He had at one time put an advertisement in the local paper under the name of 'Dr Haller' which had merely been a ruse to get an attractive young girl to respond to the advertisement, when he would ask her to meet him in Linz, where he would hire a room and attempt to drug her and then commit rape. According to the police they had had several complaints about a bogus doctor, whom they were now anxious to get their hands on.

There is no doubt that Hofrichter was a thoroughly evil man. But whether or not he was guilty of murder is another matter.

What is surprising is that his wife remained loyal to him. She was convinced of his innocence, but what she found difficult to accept was his long list of infidelities. 'I have always known him to be a liar,' she said. 'What hurt me, though, more than anything else, was the discovery of his intrigues with other women. He hid these from me by telling me when he was absent that he was going off on a shooting expedition with his comrades.'

A Colonel Kutschere of the General Staff was then called in to investigate the matter. 'Someone seems to be trying to kill the entire High Command,' the Emperor told him. 'Find the guilty man before it is too late.'

The Colonel set to work, and eventually his investigations led him to Lieutenant Hofrichter. Although he had been released from prison in Vienna through lack of evidence, he was arrested again, while serving in the nearby town of Linz. Two cardboard boxes, the same as those used in the packages Hofrichter had sent out, a mimeograph and a number of capsules were found in his quarters. After this it hardly seems necessary to add that he was also a keen amateur photographer, with access to potassium cyanide.

He was brought before no less a person than the Emperor Franz Josef, who wasted no time in coming to the point. 'You have disgraced the High Command,' he informed Lieutenant Hofrichter. 'In the circumstances, there is only one thing left for you to do, and that is to commit suicide.'

'I am sorry, sire,' said Hofrichter, 'but I am innocent, and I must therefore refuse your request. If I am deemed to be guilty I must ask for a trial before a jury.'

Hofrichter got his wish – and for his pains was sentenced to twenty years in prison, after having appeared before a military tribunal in June 1910. What helped them to decide he was guilty was the fact that one of the letters he had sent to an intended victim had been misspelled in the same way as it had been on a list of officers posted to Linz and written by him. His case had been further damaged when it was made known that he had committed a number of serious crimes under the name of Haller.

The Lieutenant was duly sent to prison, but this was far from being the end of the case. In 1918, the Austro-Hungarian Empire collapsed. The years continued to roll by, until in 1935, a Viennese solicitor happened to be reading through some legal papers which dealt with the case of Hofrichter. The more he read the more he became convinced that he was innocent.

Further inquiries revealed that he was still alive and was by now a free man, though living in extreme poverty. The solicitor became so involved with the case that he was prompted to write a play about it. The play was a sensation, and when the curtain fell on the opening night, there were calls for the author and for Hofrichter. The latter did not appear, although he had attended the performance. Instead, he slipped quietly out of a back door, returning to obscurity, never to be seen in public again.

The true facts of the case remain a mystery to this day, as there were undoubtedly questions that remained un-answered. Was Hofrichter really guilty, as the evidence suggests, or was he the innocent victim of an attempt to bring down the Austro-Hungarian Empire?

Certainly there were things about the affair which left

many people unsatisfied with the outcome. In the first place, although the search of his quarters had produced the pills and a number of boxes which he swore had been bought to house his wife's trinkets, and the capsules were found to contain a compound for worming dogs, there was some truth in the argument that many people put forward, that no one in their right mind would have held on to such incriminating items.

What really told against him was the knowledge that had come to their attention of Hofrichter's double life, when he had masqueraded as Dr Haller and led a life of debauchery. It was probably more for this reason than any other that he had been tried by a court-martial, rather than in a civil court, with the result that there was something of an uproar at the time over this decision.

The fact that Hofrichter made a confession does not mean a great deal, as he withdrew it almost immediately after he had made it.

WHO MURDERED
LIEUTENANT CHEVIS?

One of the strangest cases is the still unsolved murder of Lieutenant Hubert George Chevis, who met his end on 21 June 1931. What is so strange about this case is the seemingly complete lack of motive for the killing. A married man with two children, he occupied a bungalow on Blackdown Camp, near Aldershot, but it was only used by the whole family at weekends. For the rest of the week he stayed in the bungalow alone, while his wife and children returned to their home in London.

They led a very ordinary existence, making the most of their weekends, which played a prominent part in their lives. They were particularly looking forward to the weekend of 21 June, which happened to be the weekend of the Aldershot Tattoo, which they all intended to go to. They decided to celebrate by having a few friends in for drinks before having a family dinner after the guests had left. Lieutenant Chevis ordered a brace of partridge from the local poulterer, which he eventually handed over to his cook, Mrs Yeomans, to prepare for their evening meal.

Mrs Yeomans cleaned the birds and hung them in the ventilated meat safe outside until the late afternoon, when she transferred them to the oven. While the birds were gently cooking away, the lieutenant and his wife entertained their friends, and when the guests had finally left, the family sat down to eat, waited on by the lieutenant's batman, Private Nicholas Bulger.

As the birds were brought to the table, Lieutenant Chevis leaned forward in keen anticipation, and after Mrs Chevis had expertly carved the partridges and placed some portions on their plates, he lifted a forkful of the bird to his mouth, only to put it down again with a wry grimace.

'This is terrible!' he exclaimed.

Mrs Chevis then tasted a little of hers, carefully touching it with the tip of her tongue. 'It tastes fusty,' she said, pushing her plate aside. 'Don't eat any more of it, or you might make yourself ill.'

Hubert Chevis was still complaining bitterly about the birds when he suddenly felt an agonising cramp in his legs. Within a few minutes his legs had lost all sense of feeling, and this was followed by a violent fit of convulsions.

As the army hospital was close by he was in there in less than half an hour, where they fought to save him until the early hours of the morning, when he finally expired in one last set of violent convulsions. By now Mrs Chevis had also been taken ill, but fortunately, having had only the merest taste of one of the birds, she quickly responded to treatment, and eventually recovered.

The police were informed of the lieutenant's death as a matter of routine, and a post-mortem was arranged to be followed by an inquest. So far, it was nothing more than a tragic fatality due to accidental poisoning, or so everyone thought.

The coroner's court returned an open verdict, but as Lieutenant Chevis' father, Sir William Chevis, was preparing for his son's funeral, he received a telegram which read simply: 'Hooray, hooray, hooray!' It was signed J. Hartigan and was posted from a Dublin hotel. It was only natural that Sir William should at first think that the telegram had been sent as a joke in the worst possible taste. When he communicated with the police and showed them the telegram, they took an extremely serious view of the matter. Their forebodings about the telegram were more than fully justified as it happened. Within a few days, Sir William Chevis received another telegram, this time from Belfast, again signed by J. Hartigan, which read: 'It is a mystery they will never solve.' It was now perfectly obvious to Sir William that his son had been murdered, a view that was certainly shared by the police in Dublin, who moved with alacrity. First they interviewed all the staff and guests at the Hibernian Hotel, which was the name of the hotel given on the first telegram. They eliminated any connections between the hotel and anyone named Hartigan. They also interviewed the post office clerk who had sent the message and remembered the person who had sent it. Furthermore, they managed to identify this man as being the same person who had bought a certain amount of strychnine from a Dublin chemist.

At this point the police had been hopeful that they would find the killer quickly. But then the trail had ended abruptly, with the chemist informing them that he could give them no further information on the man who had bought the poison. This left the police exactly where they had been to begin with, without a shred of evidence or motive for the killing.

The inquest on Lieutenant Chevis was reopened at the coroner's court on 11 August, with almost nothing further to add as to the reason why he had died. The coroner opened the proceedings by going over the already known facts about the case, which must have seemed like a statement of the obvious to Sir William Chevis, who was still utterly baffled as to the reason for his son's mysterious death.

The coroner made a point of criticising the *Daily Sketch* for having published, without permission, a copy of the 'Hooray' telegram, which had prompted J. Hartigan to send the newspaper a telegram which read: 'Dear Sir, Why do you publish a picture of the Hooray telegram? J. Hartigan.' This telegram no doubt increased the sales of the newspaper enormously, but it certainly brought them no nearer to solving the mystery.

Witnesses were also called to tell the jury what part they had played in the mysterious death of Lieutenant Chevis. Neither Bulger, the batman, nor Mrs Yeomans could throw any light on the matter, beyond going into how they had served the partridges. There was one startling moment, however, and that was when the batman admitted the fact that he had been born in Ireland. This proved to have no relevance to the case beyond the fact that the telegrams had been sent from Ireland and the police were back where they began.

All that was left for the coroner to do was to present the jury with the known facts of the case, which were precious few; the main fact being that Lieutenant Chevis had died from asphyxia following strychnine poisoning, and that it had been administered by placing it in the flesh of the partridges.

The jury took only five minutes to return an open verdict, and that verdict still stands to this day on this strange episode.

With this case now almost forgotten, it might be interesting to go into some of the reasons why the murder might have occurred. First of all, it is worth looking at the type of poison which was used in the killing. All deaths by poisoning are a ghastly experience for the victim, particularly for those who have been killed with a dose of strychnine. Death occurs in extreme agony with a series of violent convulsions, after the victim has already been deprived of his reason.

That is why poison is often known as the coward's weapon, and seems to have been used as a murder method mainly by women; it is also a method which needs only as little as half a grain to murder anyone in less than twenty minutes.

But in this case, no other woman was known to be involved, unless one includes Mrs Yeomans, who was clearly innocent anyway. Nor, on the surface of it, was there any possibility that Lieutenant Chevis had been having an affair with a vengeful lover. He was a happily married man who always got on well with his wife and children. Besides, there was the anonymous person who had sent the 'Hooray' telegram.

Among the unlikely suspects there was Private Bulger, who had always got on well with the lieutenant, because he had always treated him as an equal. Is it possible that he was an undercover agent of the IRA? This seems extremely unlikely, as the IRA have never made any secret of their killings.

It seems to me, at least, that there was only one possible solution to the mystery. In all probability Lieutenant Chevis was not a murder victim at all, but was merely the unhappy casualty of a bird that had been feeding on berries containing strychnine, and had later been killed and despatched among a consignment sent to his local poulterer.

To claim that Chevis was murdered deliberately makes no sense at all, especially when one bears in mind that his wife might well have been the first to have tasted some of the bird, or even fully eaten it, in which case the alleged murderer would have claimed the wrong victim.

As to the mysterious telegram sent to Sir William, this was probably nothing more than a cruel hoax which might have been sent by one of his ex-soldiers who had read of the death of Lieutenant Chevis in the national newspapers, and had then decided to inflict a malicious joke on Sir William.

The only possible alternative to the theory of the poison-bearing partridge is that Chevis became lonely staying by himself in the bungalow while his wife was away, and may have had an affair with a local girl who had got fed up with the whole situation, and had put strychnine in the bird while it was in the meat safe, in which case she wouldn't have minded too much if his wife had also poisoned herself.

THE
KILLER PLAYBOY

Known to the press at one time as the 'sexual deviant
playboy', Wayne Lonergan was a personable-looking
young man from Toronto who had become bored with his
home town and decided to move to New York, where he
hoped to take up residence in Manhattan, where the money
was. He arrived there in 1939, the year of the World's Fair,
when there were all manner of jobs available for anyone
who was prepared to work long hours for good money. At
that time Wayne was undeterred by hard work and to begin
with he got himself a job as a salesman in the menswear
department of Abercrombie and Fitch, the main attraction
being the handsome bonus he got in the shape of being able
to buy anything he wanted at a large discount. Being a natty
dresser he took the opportunity of replenishing his whole
wardrobe.

In the following year he went to work for a well-known
photographer named Anton Bruehl, who ran his agency
from a set of offices in the old Grand Central Palace
Building. Wayne liked the job, and for a while he worked
hard at it. After a few months, however, he decided to
move on. It was while he was between jobs that it suddenly

dawned on him that a presentable young man like himself didn't have to work. Almost overnight he turned himself into something of a con man, earning a living of sorts by existing on his wits.

He met Patricia Burton in the winter of 1940 and began taking her out. She was eighteen at the time and was a quiet girl with a pretty face and a charming manner which Wayne found completely captivating. She may have seemed inexperienced, which in some ways she was, but she was nevertheless far from being as innocent as she looked. She had spent a great deal of time on the Riviera and travelled around in the company of young men who were full of small talk and precious little else. The only thing they had to recommend them to Wayne was that all of them without exception were stinking rich. To be fair to Wayne, he did not try to exploit his new friends, but he was something of a hanger-on at their parties, to which he was generally invited to make up the numbers.

Strangely enough, Patricia seems to have taken a liking to Wayne, who must have seemed distinctly wet behind the ears compared to her more sophisticated friends.

It was about this time also that he encountered Patricia's father, William O. Burton, in the lobby of the Gramercy Park Hotel. He seems to have taken an instant liking to Lonergan, and in no time at all he had him set up in an apartment, and had also provided him with a handsome allowance. It was therefore hardly surprising that the rumours began to fly about that the two of them were engaged in a homosexual relationship.

If this indeed were the case, Patricia took the affair

between Wayne and her father with remarkable composure. After all, it is not every day that you come across a case where daughter and father are both sleeping with the same man!

William O. Burton was an interesting man. Forty years old when he met Lonergan, he was a self-made man who had travelled widely aboard his yacht while making the Riviera his base for a number of years before returning to New York, with the hold of his yacht crammed with art treasures.

One would have thought that the situation over Wayne Lonergan would have been fraught with difficulties, but strangely enough they all seemed to get on well together, and there is no record of them quarrelling.

There was only one fly in the ointment, and that was Patricia's mother, Mrs Lucile Burton, who had fought hard to keep the young lovers apart, and had spent years in her husband's company until she had finally managed to get a legal separation from him. Now living in reduced circumstances in an apartment in the Hotel Elysée, she spent much of her time hounding Wayne and her daughter, to say nothing of William Burton, who was busy waging his private war against his ex-wife.

Then quite suddenly the whole situation changed overnight, when William Burton died unexpectedly from a heart attack, leaving the yacht to Patricia and precious little else, so that she was obliged to sell it at a fraction of its value.

Later in the week one of the family lawyers paid Wayne a brief visit and warned him that as they would be selling the apartment, it would be advisable to remove any of the items he wished to keep as soon as possible.

Patricia and Wayne were seeing each other almost every day now that there was no Burton Snr around to make demands on Wayne's time. Mostly they met at Pat's insistence as she was trying to avoid one of the many suitors that her mother was setting up for her. In the end she got so tired of it all that she put it on the line for Wayne. 'Okay, let's get married,' she said. 'We could go down to Reno some time next week.'

Lonergan, who was looking for a new abode which would cost him nothing, was delighted at the suggestion, and in the summer of 1943 he moved to a townhouse at 983 Park Avenue, where Patricia sublet three floors. The rest she kept for their own use.

After living in some style at the apartment supplied by Mr Burton, Wayne must have found his new living accommodation something of a comedown, but the furnishings, though somewhat heavy, exuded an air of solid respectability, and the house was in a good neighbourhood. So it suited Lonergan, who was grateful to be living at an expensive address rent free.

Having got this far, it seems surprising that so early in the relationship, Wayne had decided that their marriage was not going to work. Already they had agreed that they were more or less going to lead separate lives. To this end he joined the Royal Canadian Air Force; Canada was preparing to enter the Second World War. He had gone back to Canada briefly in order to join up, but the authorities had not exactly acted with lightning speed, with the result that he was still waiting to be called up.

In actual fact, he did not get his papers until September

1943, and it was at some time during that month that he had lunch with the family lawyer, who told him that Patricia wanted a divorce, but that the legal fees for a fight in court would be staggering. For that reason Wayne decided not to contest the case. The main thing, after all, was to walk away from the divorce with as little cost to himself as possible.

It does seem strange though, given Wayne's preoccupation with easy money, that he should have been seriously considering divorce. With Pat's income of $25,000 a year, one would have thought that Wayne would have made some attempt to preserve the marriage, especially as they now had a son who had been born in April 1942. But in many ways Lonergan was an unpredictable man, who did not seem to have his own interests at heart for much of the time.

On Saturday 23 October 1943, he went to the home of his friend, John Frederick Hajes, arriving in the early hours of the morning. Wayne Lonergan was by now an Aircraftman, and had obtained a forty-eight-hour pass from his RCAF school in Toronto.

After breakfast Hajes informed Wayne that he could have the flat all to himself as he was going to the country for the weekend. He watched something of the Navy Day parade and then went off to the world-famous toy shop, F. A. O. Schwartz, to buy a present for his son. He then filled in the rest of the day by keeping a lunch appointment. His evening was to be taken up seeing the latest musical starring Mary Martin and John Boles; his companion was a Mrs Jaburg, an extremely attractive woman who had spent a number of years behind the footlights working under the name of Jean Murphy. They were 'just good friends' as the saying goes, and there was certainly nothing sexual about their relationship.

From then on nothing is known about Wayne's movements that night. Presumably, after he had seen Mrs Jaburg home, he had gone to the flat where Hajes lived and turned in for the night.

As for Patricia, we know that she had gone out with a middle-aged man named Mario Enzo Gabellini, an interior decorator whom she had already met on a couple of occasions and who had something of a reputation for being a fast worker with the ladies. This seems to be borne out by the fact that he had picked her up that evening at the Peter Cooper Hotel.

Later that night they were supposed to meet Thomas Farrell, the editor of a low-grade women's magazine, who was to be accompanied by a female friend. Farrell and his girlfriend turned up eventually, and the four of them went to dinner. At the end of the night out, it was Gabellini who took Patricia home sometime around 6 a.m.

On the night of Sunday 24 October, Elizabeth Black, the Lonergan nanny and her friend, Peter Elser, were both concerned that Patricia had not appeared all day. They broke into her room and found her naked body lying on the bed. She had been bludgeoned and then strangled to death.

Dr Milton Helpern, the deputy medical examiner arrived on the scene and briefly examined the body, whereupon he told the police that death had been caused by Patricia having been struck repeatedly over the head with an onyx-inlaid candlestick and then strangled.

The police quickly dismissed Gabellini from their list of possible suspects, which left Wayne as their prime suspect. Of course, there was always the possibility that Patricia had been murdered by some unknown killer, especially as there had been a number of murders in the area she had lived in over the last year or so. All they knew for certain was that she had been killed after she had hung up her clothes that night before preparing for bed. As the bed had never been slept in one presumes that her attacker killed her before she had time to retire.

When the police got around to looking for Lonergan it was to learn that he was in Toronto, which he visited from time to time. On the night of the 24th he had just returned to the apartment he still maintained, when there was a sharp knock on the door. It was the Toronto police, who had come to arrest him for Patricia's murder. They then took him down to headquarters, where two detectives from New York were waiting to escort him back there.

He arrived at La Guardia Airport in the early hours of the morning of 27 October. One of the incriminating things against him was the presence of two scratches on his face, which the police maintained could have been made by Patricia while fighting for her life. For twenty-four hours he was grilled mercilessly in the shabby police building in downtown New York. By the Thursday morning they had questioned him for something like seventy-two hours and in that time he had had less than four hours' sleep. In the early hours of that Thursday morning he broke. After his confession he surrendered his braces to prevent any possible suicide bid and was hustled down to a cell, where he stretched himself out on the bed and fell asleep within a few seconds.

In his confession, Wayne had stated that he had got rid of

his bloodstained uniform by stowing it in his duffel bag and throwing it into the Hudson River. Despite repeated dredgings of the river, it was never found.

Another unsatisfying element in this story is the testimony of a GI named Maurice Worcester, who was supposed to have made the scratches on Wayne's chin, rather than Patricia. 'Look,' he stated. 'I have taught ju-jitsu and have fought all my life. Do you really think he would have come out with only a couple of scratches on the chin if he had fought with me?'

At first Wayne Lonergan had been portrayed by the press with some sympathy, but overnight he was turned into a contemptible figure and a sexual deviant of the worst order. Now that the press had done its bit, the rest was left to the court to put the final touches at the trial which began on the morning of 23 February 1944. The press had a field day with stories of homosexual orgies about to be revealed for the first time and which involved the names of many well-known people. One of the worst and most vicious of the journalists was Thyra Samter Winslow, who claimed to have knowledge of a number of these orgies which she wrote of in the *Mirror*.

One way and another there was so much animosity now being directed at Wayne that everything appeared stacked against him and it is difficult to imagine how he could have had a fair trial. No one seems to have had any qualms about how the 'confession' had been extracted from Wayne in the first place, who had only 'confessed' when he had reached a state of mind when he would have been willing to sign anything as long as he was allowed to sleep. Nor could anyone have survived the countless venomous attacks that had been launched against him without some of the dirt rubbing off on him.

His defence lawyer tried to redress the balance to some degree by having a psychiatrist claim that Lonergan was a psychopathic personality, and could not therefore be judged by ordinary standards. None of this made any difference. On 17 April 1944, he was found guilty and convicted of second-degree murder. He was sentenced to thirty years in prison. He served all but nine years of it in Clinton State Prison in Dannemora, New York, before being let out on parole on 2 December 1965, and was subsequently deported to Canada on the understanding that he would not return to the United States ever again without the specific permission of the US authorities.

The interest in this case is not whether or not Lonergan was guilty, but in the way the press and the authorities unwittingly conspired to judge a man guilty without having heard a shred of evidence against him apart from his admission that he had called on Patricia that night, when he had killed her in a fit of uncontrollable rage. If they had listened a little more and accused a little less readily, the final verdict on Lonergan might have been less severe than it was.

THE CASE OF
THE DECOY TELEGRAM

Thomas Henry Allaway was a grim-faced man with a permanently sullen expression who was often seen around Bournemouth, generally in his smart double-breasted chauffeur's uniform and peaked cap. To say that he took a pride in his uniform would be an exaggeration, but there was no doubt that he was even more arrogant than usual when wearing it. Perhaps it was the car which made him more arrogant towards people when he was driving it. The car was a Mercedes and was the property of a Mr and Mrs Sutton of Barton Close, Bournemouth.

During the war he had been in the Royal Army Service Corps, but had deserted early on. On his recapture he was sent back to France, and from there he had moved on to active service on the Rhine. He had a mouth which always seemed half open, which did nothing for his general appearance, giving him an unpleasant demeanour. It is therefore somewhat surprising to learn that someone had nevertheless found him attractive enough to marry him.

Meanwhile, the inhabitants of Bournemouth had been shocked to hear that their pleasant seaside town had been

123

the scene of a murder. In the early hours of the morning on 23 December, a labourer named Nicklen had been walking to work down the Iford–Tuckton Lane between Bournemouth and Christchurch when he became aware of three cows nosing around something that lay in the middle of a field. When he went over to see what was attracting their attention, to his horror he saw that it was the body of a young woman whose nether garments had been violently disarranged.

He turned and stumbled back the way he had come and reported the matter to the police, and by nine o'clock the police surgeon had arrived on the scene, when only the briefest of examinations told him that she had been murdered while trying to defend herself. Further inquiries about the dead woman revealed that she was Irene Wilkins, who lived in Streatham and had come to Bournemouth after receiving an answer to her advertisement asking for a post as cook.

When the police went to interview the dead girl's mother, she showed them a telegram which told her to come to Bournemouth Central Station, where a car would be waiting for her. It was a promising sign for the future that there was a rider to the telegram which said: 'Expense no object.' It was signed in the name of Wood and was sent from Beech House.

According to her mother, Irene had been looking forward to going after the job as a cook, which she was convinced she would get. She had served with the Women's Auxiliary Corps during the war and was bored with civilian life. Now aged thirty-one, she was convinced that this new life opening up for her could well lead to something that might even have marriage prospects attached to it.

It was the year of 1921, and people were not as suspicious of such advertisements as they are today. She had therefore gone off with the highest of hopes, only to have them shattered when the murderer had lured her to her death.

As it happened, Irene Wilkins had been noticed by a Mr Frank Humphris, who had travelled down from London on the 4.30 train on 22 December and had happened to see someone answering to Irene's description standing outside the station looking around her. As he was watching her, a gust of wind blew up and picked up a number of newspapers from a pile nearby. Mr Humphris ran forward to intercept them and almost knocked over a man dressed in a chauffeur's uniform. The chauffeur met the woman and together the two of them got into a greenish-grey car and drove off. He did not notice the make.

The case was now being supervised by Superintendent Garrett, who had been working hard with what little evidence he had available. First he had spent some time studying the decoy telegram and had noticed that several words had been misspelled. They were the sort of mistakes which would have been made by a poorly educated man. This was undoubtedly evidence of a sort, but which could only be of value if the murderer were asked to write out the telegram again and were to make the same mistakes.

A further piece of more solid evidence came from Mr Humphris, who had seen the car a second time, when he made a point of taking down the registration number, which was LK7403, and had passed it on to Garrett who had checked it out and found that the car belonged to Mr

Sutton of Barton Close, Southborough. The car's registration records also included the name of the family chauffeur – Thomas Henry Allaway.

Garrett was already quite convinced that Allaway was the man who had been responsible for the death of Irene Wilkins. Once Christmas was over, he decided to pull in Allaway for vigorous questioning, which would probably end in his arrest. But there was only one problem: Allaway was no longer to be found at his home, or at his place of work. And for that matter he was not at his wife's house either.

'How about money?' Garrett asked Mrs Allaway. 'Did he have enough to keep him going for a few days?'

His wife shook her head tearfully. 'He had almost nothing. As usual, he had lost whatever he might have had on the horses.'

As it happened, as Garrett learned later, Allaway had some twenty pounds in his pocket, having gone off with Mr Sutton's cheque book. He had then forged three cheques, which had been readily accepted by the local tradesmen who had known him well enough to trust him.

Allaway was now very much a wanted man, and it was for this reason that he was quickly spotted by a local policeman in Reading, who approached him. Allaway made off in an attempt to escape, but fortunately a passer-by had also recognised him and was quick enough to trip him up as he ran past.

He spent the night in a police cell in Reading and was taken back the next morning under escort to Bournemouth.

Mrs Allaway was asked to attend the Bournemouth

police station, and to bring with her a letter written in her husband's handwriting. The letter she brought with her to the station was not in the same upright script used on the telegram, but it contained the same spelling mistakes that Garrett had noticed on the telegram. A feeble excuse was put forward by Allaway, who said that the letter to his wife was not written by him as he had injured his hand at the time it was written. This was so easily disproved that his defence was in shreds from the start. In fact, Allaway had spent some time practising the upright hand he used for the telegram in a vain effort at disguising the identity of the sender.

And that was only the beginning.

A week later he was put in a line-up with a number of other men, and was immediately identified as the man that several witnesses had seen on the day of the murder.

Allaway was then asked by Garrett if he would care to make a statement, and after hesitating for a few moments, he agreed to write one out for him, which he did in a sloping hand which bore no relation to the upright one used on the telegram. The statement was written in an illiterate scrawl which purported to go over the events of what was supposed to have occurred on the day of the murder, and which was a pack of lies from beginning to end. His story was that he had not been in the Mercedes at the time of the murder, nor had he driven to Bournemouth Central Station on that same day.

Despite all his frantic wriggling to get out of the situation in which he had placed himself, Thomas Henry Allaway was put on trial for murder at the Winchester Assizes on 3 July 1922. He found himself facing Mr Justice Avory, a well-known figure on the Bench, and a man who had a reputation as a fair judge.

The case started badly for Allaway when Mr Frank Humphris was called to the witness box from where he looked across to Allaway and stated that he recognised him as the man he had seen at Bournemouth Central Station on the day of the murder. This was only the first of a stream of damning witnesses who had been called to give evidence. Not one of them had a good word to say in his favour. It was by then quite obvious that his case was a hopeless one.

Mr Justice Avory finally summed up in his usual impartial manner, and mentioned in passing the fair treatment that had been given him by the handwriting expert who had been called in.

'No expert could have presented his evidence in a more proper and reputable manner than he did,' Mr Avory said. 'Of course,' he added reasonably. 'You are not bound by his conclusions – namely that the telegram was written by the same person and that that person is the prisoner.'

The jury were of the same opinion as the handwriting expert, and an hour later they returned to the courtroom with a verdict of guilty. As a result Allaway was sentenced to death by hanging.

The night before his execution he confessed to the prison governor, while only the previous night, when he had been visited by his wife and his brother, who had turned up on one of his rare visits, he had told them both that he was innocent of the crime.

Allaway appealed against the verdict, but was turned down. On the morning of 19 August 1922, he was led out to keep his appointment with William Ellis, the executioner.

It was at this point that the awful majesty of the law broke down. Allaway was pinioned and then took his position on the drop, when something went horribly wrong. As Allaway fell through the trap door, the noose slipped slightly and instead of him falling to what should have been his immediate death by having his neck broken, he died an agonising death by strangulation instead. By the time Ellis had realised that something had gone hideously wrong, Allaway had finally died. Once it was ascertained that he *was* dead, he was left to hang there overnight, as was the custom.

It would be easy to say that Thomas Henry Allaway had died a death that was certainly no worse than the one he had meted out to Irene Wilkins. But when things went wrong as they did in this case, it was a sad reflection on the law as it stood then, underlining its barbarity.

The last public hanging was in 1868, and up to that time an execution meant death by slow strangulation at best. After that date, a more humane method of hanging was used, and a condemned criminal was despatched as quickly and painlessly as possible. At least it was a step in the right direction.

THE MAN
WHO WOULDN'T DIE

In the years immediately preceding the First World War,
New York was a crooked city, probably far more so than it
is today. It was a city where corruption was rife, so much so
that even most of its police force was suspect. The worst
offender was Lieutenant Charles Becker, who was involved
in every form of graft and corruption going. Like so many
of his fellow officers, he had dealings with all sorts of
unwholesome characters, including one by the name of
Herman Rosenthal, who was convinced that everyone in
the police was against him and was trying to get a journalist
named Herbert Swope to write a series of exposés
concerning the corruption in the force, and had already
sworn an affidavit to that effect. The fact that Swope was
being supported by Lieutenant Becker in this was purely
because Becker wanted to make a good impression on the
District Attorney, Charles Whitman.

Now Rosenthal had made a statement saying that he
intended to name a policeman in connection with the
corrupt practices going on in the city. This had made him
very much a marked man in New York, where life was held
cheaply in certain quarters. Rosenthal's almost pathological

attacks on the officer amused most people. Others saw him as a dangerous menace, not the least of them being Charles Becker, who realised that Rosenthal had to be silenced as soon as possible if he was not to threaten his future. Becker could see all too clearly the privileged position he had built up for himself being in danger. He decided that the only possible thing for him to do was to remove Rosenthal.

It was for this reason that Rosenthal found himself faced one morning with four ruthless killers who shot him down in cold blood. Five bullets in all were pumped into him. Rosenthal's murder was to cost four men their lives in the electric chair, and yet another was shot in reprisal for the killing behind the bar of his saloon in East North Street.

The murder also had its repercussions in other areas. It put an end to the political career of the mayor of the city, it made Herbert Swope the best-known journalist in the country and it halted the total control of the city by the hoodlum element. From that point onwards the gangster brethren would never be quite the same.

It was some time after Rosenthal's killing that someone remembered he had a wife. Two journalists, more in search of an angle than anything, raced over to Rosenthal's house, where they broke the news of his death to Mrs Rosenthal.

'I begged him not to go,' she sobbed. 'But he wouldn't listen. Apart from anything else he said he had an appointment that day that he had to keep.'

Such was the impact of the murder that it occupied the headlines for several days. During that time, Becker, in the company of an Inspector Hughes, had examined the corpse. When they returned to the station they found a line-up in progress. Needless to say, no fresh evidence turned up. How could it, when the guilty man was walking away right before their eyes?

But Charles Becker's position was not as safe as he thought. As it happened, the district attorney had already decided that Charles Becker was the man who had committed the murder, and he had the word put round that he was willing to offer immunity to anyone who would help him convict Becker.

It was not so long after that he received a visit from Bald Jack Rose, a well-known underworld character, who strolled into the police station while Herman Rosenthal was being buried. He made a thirty-eight-page confession, naming Becker as the man who had ordered him to hire the killers responsible for Rosenthal's death.

A few days later, Deputy Police Commissioner Dougherty called on District Attorney Whitman. 'Well, do you want me to arrest Lieutenant Becker?' he demanded.

Whitman shook his head. 'Not yet.'

Dougherty sighed. 'All right. At least we agree as to who is at the back of the killing.'

Becker was finally arrested eight days later. In the meantime, Whitman had strengthened his hand by getting another gangster named Sam Schepps to agree to testify against Becker in exchange for having all criminal charges dropped against him. Becker had already been shown to be a sub-human creature by the evidence so far collected and his future before a jury looked none too bright.

But it was really Bald Jack Rose who was Whitman's star witness. In his famous statement he had openly admitted to the 'Croak Rosenthal decree' issued by Becker. The four killers who had been responsible for Herman Rosenthal's death were all convicted in the space of twenty minutes and went to the electric chair on 13 April 1914.

Becker, though, was still the main enemy as far as Whitman was concerned, and he had now taken it upon himself to make sure he was convicted. Becker, on the other hand, was serenely convinced as to what the outcome of the trial would be. After all, as he was fond of telling anyone who would listen, what reasonable jury would believe the gangster trash Whitman was proposing to put on the stand rather than an upright police officer like himself?

Whitman's war of attrition against Becker was temporarily halted when a hoodlum named Jack Zelig was murdered. His killer had jumped on the running board of his car and had killed him with a well-placed bullet behind Zelig's left ear. The murder, which had been carried out by a gangster named 'Red Phil' Davidson was completely unrelated to the Becker case, but it caused a small break in Whitman's concentration on it, while he brought Davidson to trial for a murder for which, incidentally, he was given twenty-one years' imprisonment.

Becker eventually went on trial in front of Judge John Goff, a man who had an impeccable record when it came to dealing with graft and corruption. Generally a scrupulously fair man, he was so obviously prejudiced against the accused that he gave Whitman every opportunity to put forward his case, while giving Becker's defence lawyer no leeway on anything. At the end of the trial Becker said feelingly to him: 'Between that judge and your inability to stop the DA, I'm going to fry! I could have done better myself.'

Despite his hostility towards the judge and his defence counsel, Becker was still convinced that the case for the prosecution would not stand up in court, and that it would seem to the jury that this was an example of an unfair trial. He told his wife that he was so confident of the outcome in court that the two of them would go out that evening to dinner. No one was therefore more shocked than he when the jury brought in a verdict of guilty. Fortunately for him the Appeals Court overturned the conviction.

Becker's second trial, which began on 2 May 1914, was held before Judge Seabury. This time there was no mistake. From the beginning the judge made his own position clear. In the dock Becker sat ready and waiting for the verdict. He must even at this stage been quite sure what the outcome would be, as he sat there in complete control of the situation.

The clerk of the court put forward the question: 'Gentleman of the jury, have you agreed on your verdict?'

'Guilty as charged in the indictment,' came back the answer in little more than a whisper.

It must be said that to Becker's credit there was hardly a flicker of emotion on his face as he listened to the verdict being read out, and the sentence of death passed on him.

It was over at last. For fear of reprisals by the hostile crowds he was driven to Sing Sing in the sheriff's own car. It was only then that Becker's iron control began to slip when he realised fully what was going to happen to him. Pulling himself together, he alighted from the car and walked with a firm tread to his cell.

Late in February 1915, a 540-page brief was submitted to the Court of Appeals. The arguments put forward in it were that the trial was manifestly unfair and had been conducted in a manner hostile to the defendant and was highly prejudicial to his rights.

The Court of Appeals judgement was handed down on 25 May, just a year after Becker's second conviction. The court's ruling came down squarely against Becker. The execution was set down as due to take place on 16 July. In all it had taken the court three years to bring matters up to this point. When the news was given to Becker some time later in the afternoon of that day, he seemed to have accepted the inevitable.

Earlier, on 1 January 1915, Whitman was made Governor of the State of New York, a fact that Becker made a wistful reference to when the date of his execution neared. 'I suppose there's no chance of a reprieve coming through from him? But there wouldn't be, would there? I've never known a case yet where the public prosecutor won the death sentence, only for the prisoner to win his freedom from him at a later date.'

Only twelve hours before he was due to die, his wife went to Whitman's office and begged to see him. He agreed to see her at the Governor's mansion in Albany, but when she arrived it was to find that he had gone off somewhere to view a military event, even though he had promised he would be there to receive her. She eventually cornered him the same day, when he had to admit that there was nothing he could do.

By then it was almost time for Becker to walk to the electric chair. It was 30 July when he left his cell and made his way under escort to the death room at Sing Sing. The official invitations had been sent out and their recipients were now waiting to see Charles Becker die. Becker entered the death chamber and stared around at the twenty-two witnesses that were gathered solemnly before him. He approached the electric chair and sat down on it without any assistance. He repeated the litany by Father James Curry, who then stood back to allow justice to take its course.

A broad strap was pulled across his mouth, at which point the executioner threw the switch that sent 1,850 volts through Charles Becker's body. When the switch was pulled back and the body examined, it was found that Becker's heart was not only still beating, but thumping away strongly. The switch was thrown again, but the doctor once more reported that Becker was still alive. He was then given another ten-second jolt, and this time when the doctor examined him and listened to his heart, he said: 'This man is dead.'

The execution was one of the most botched in the history of Sing Sing. The truth of the matter was that Becker had been in perfect health, without any spare flesh on his body, and being in such a fit condition it had been difficult to finish him off as cleanly as would have been wished.

His wife, loyal to the last, handed over a statement for distribution to the press. It read:

I shall never rest until I have exposed the methods used to convict my husband. Whether he was guilty or innocent, there was never any justification for the means employed to convict him. In all the ten years of our married life I never had occasion to regret I was his wife. He was not an angel, he never made a pretence of being one. He was just an ordinary human being, and that is why I loved him so much.

Helen Becker.

It was an epitaph of which Charles Becker would have been proud. Whether he deserved any of it is another matter.

THE
FATAL ATTRACTION

Susan Christie came from a typical middle-class background, and had been brought up with a respect for law and order. She had the usual middle-class morals, which included not giving herself cheaply to the first man that came along. All this makes her behaviour with Captain Duncan McAllister, a married man who was serving with the Royal Corps of Signals in Ireland, so out of keeping with everything she had been taught.

She had fallen in love with him almost from their first meeting, and he had reciprocated her advances in the only way he knew how, and that was by sleeping with her as frequently as possible. To give Captain McAllister credit, he had made it clear from the beginning that he had no intention of leaving his wife for her. If he was hoping that a little honesty at the outset would perhaps make life easier in the long run, he was to get some rude shocks along the way. In this case, a little bland lying, reprehensible though it might have been, could well have saved Penny McAllister's life.

Instead, we had a situation where a twenty-three-year-old girl with no knowledge of the world was madly in love with a man for whom she would be prepared to do anything, given half a chance, and all of whose waking hours were given over to thoughts of him when she was not carrying out her duties for the Ulster Defence Regiment in Portadown.

Oddly enough, she was on quite good terms with the wife. This was probably because they were all members of the aqua club which had been organised and was now being run by Duncan McAllister. The three of them had gone for a swimming holiday on Ascension Island, where Susan and the Captain became so sexually obsessed with each other that they could not wait until they were alone, but had sex under water, while Mrs McAllister sat on the beach quite unaware of what her husband was doing.

The underwater sex was featured prominently in Susan's log book, which was also signed by McAllister, who called himself Mickey Moray, Susan's pet name for his penis. For Penny McAllister not to have guessed instinctively by now that something was going on between them shows an extraordinary naivety. On the other hand, though, why should she have suspected that something was afoot when her husband had never shown the slightest interest in other women?

As for Susan Christie, she had become totally obsessed with McAllister. When she found out that she was pregnant by him, she implored him to get rid of his wife and marry her. He repeated what he had said at the beginning of the affair that he was very fond of her, but would never dream of leaving his wife for her. Considering that he now had an hysterical woman on his hands, McAllister's stand against her seems commendable enough, but his brutal honesty must have taken her to the very edge of insanity, especially when he also told her that the only way out of her situation was for her to get rid of the baby.

For the first time Susan began seriously to plot Penny McAllister's murder, which she eventually carried out in the most horrifying manner. It was the habit of the two women to take their dogs for a walk together. On 27 March 1991 they set off to do just that in Drumkeeragh Forest Park near Ballynahinch. On this occasion Christie did not bring her dog with her, but Penny McAllister had her two golden labradors. As the dogs went bounding through the grass, Christie walked quietly behind her unsuspecting victim and drew a sharpened butcher's knife across her throat.

As Mrs McAllister fell to the ground, her throat slit almost from ear to ear, Susan Christie made a number of self-inflicted wounds on various parts of her own body. She then went in search of the police and told them that the two of them had been attacked by a sex pervert, who had first killed Mrs McAllister and then had tried to rape her.

The police refused to believe Susan Christie's story, despite the fact that for more than a year after the murder, she continued to protest her innocence, claiming that she could not recall what had happened.

When Mrs McAllister's parents, the Squires, arrived in Northern Ireland from their home in Arundel, Sussex, her mother's attitude towards Christie was openly hostile, and she was particularly upset that Christie had never once said that she was sorry.

Both Mr and Mrs Squire were particularly hurt by the press dubbing the case 'Northern Ireland's Fatal

Attraction' after the film of that name, starring Michael Douglas and Glenn Close. 'What happened to Penny was real,' Mrs Squire said, with feeling. 'I did resent the Fatal Attraction theme that kept recurring, because this was my daughter's life – not some damn film.'

Mr Squire had tried vainly to control his sobbing wife, and later had this to say of Christie: 'It is as if a disciple of the devil had come and taken some of the best things away from this world. I think that if this had been medieval times, she would have been burnt as a witch.'

To be fair to Christie she was in far too emotional a state to think of apologising for the murder of Penny McAllister. Over the last year she had reached a state of mind where she was unable to distinguish reality from fiction. Only on one thing did she remain clear, and that was her undying love for McAllister, which was now stronger than ever. Her mental state was not improved by the loss of the baby earlier in the year, brought about in all probability by the emotional turmoil and stress she was going through.

She was brought up for trial on 10 June 1992, and at the beginning she admitted to the killing, but later claimed she was suffering from diminished responsibility at the time and was therefore entering a plea of manslaughter. Quite rightly the Crown refused to accept this plea.

'I did it for Duncan,' Christie said towards the end of the trial. 'I was so much in love with him that I would have done anything for him. He was so much a part of me it was hurting. My love for him was like a drug you cannot do without.'

'Were you jealous of Mrs McAllister?' she was asked.

'Jealousy played a part in the killing, but not everything,'

142

Christie told them. 'I never saw Penny as an enemy; I saw Penny almost as a victim of my affair with Duncan. She was always so nice to me.'

When speaking of Duncan and herself, she managed to reduce the women jurors to tears, especially when she told them of her pregnancy. 'Captain McAllister wanted me to have an abortion, and later he gave me a telephone number where an appointment could be arranged.' She told the court that the affair had finally cooled and about the subsequent loss of the baby.

Realising their affair was coming to an end they had decided to have a final weekend together which they spent in the captain's married quarters while his wife was away. Before they parted, McAllister told her that the affair was at an end and that in future if they met it was to be as platonic friends.

It was only four days after their final meeting that Susan Christie had gone out and slit Mrs McAllister's throat.

It was not until the eighth day of the trial, when Dr Brown took the stand, that the whole course of the trial began to swing in Christie's favour. 'Susan had become addicted to Duncan McAllister,' he informed the court. 'Even though the relationship hurt, she kept coming back for more. I have since come to the conclusion that she was suffering from a depressive illness at the time of the killing,' Dr Brown went on gravely. 'My view is not altered by the evidence. From what she has told me, she was under serious stress, brought about by the lack of support from Captain McAllister. The symptoms she displayed, such as being in a depressed state of mind, her lack of interest, tiredness and the need for an excessive amount of sleep, were all consistent with this diagnosis. I might say that at no time did she express any anger or resentment towards Mrs McAllister.'

When asked what all this signified, Dr Brown said: 'I think it emphasises the complexity of the case and the difficulty in isolating a single motive.' Christie had constantly denied any knowledge of the killing or of the knife. 'Medical research has shown that amnesia is a feature in a considerable number of cases where people are charged with murder or manslaughter,' Dr Brown concluded. (One is tempted to add to these statements of Dr Brown, that amnesia is a very convenient way out for people in similar circumstances.)

A Dr Lyons was also called in to give evidence on Susan Christie's behalf. This was a man with thirty years' experience as a psychiatrist who informed the court that at the time of the murder she was suffering from a mental abnormality caused by her reaction to stress. He also said that this was an internationally recognised depressive disease and that it had applied particularly to Christie as she was a girl who had been under great stress stemming chiefly from her love affair with Captain McAllister. 'The major stress she suffered resulted from the secrecy of their affair and the fact that he was married and that she knew his wife,' the doctor explained.

All this, and the previous statements of Dr Brown, was in direct opposition to the remarks made by Dr Norris, also a consultant psychiatrist who gave a much more down-to-earth report after the two meetings he had with Christie. He found her to be an articulate, intelligent young woman, and on both occasions he had examined her he had

144

considered her mental state to be normal. 'Her behaviour at the examinations led me to believe that her actions were entirely appropriate to the situation. She was not depressed or unduly anxious,' he said flatly.

It was his opinion, the doctor said, that she was suffering from a mild degree of mental abnormality at the time of the killing, and he went on to state that Christie was able to form her judgements and would have known what was right or wrong.

Under cross-examination Dr Norris said he could not accept that Christie was exposed to exceptional stress in the period before the killing. 'It is my belief that she was capable of controlling her actions,' he concluded.

After what had gone before, Dr Norris's statements came like a breath of fresh air to a number of people who had listened open-mouthed to the remarks passed by Drs Brown and Lyons.

There was one final bombshell dropped at the trial, and that was when the verdict on the case was given by Lord Justice Kelly, who made the following comments before passing sentence: 'You will not be free of the burden of this crime you have committed. But I hope you will find a degree of happiness which has so far eluded you. I now sentence you to five years' imprisonment for your crime.'

The five-year sentence the judge passed on Susan Christie provoked an uproar, the consensus of opinion being that the sentence was far too lenient for the crime. Within five weeks, the Attorney General, Sir Nicholas Lyell, applied for the case to be reconsidered by the Court of Appeal in Belfast. The decision of the court was handed down on 11 November 1992. The Appeal judges heard her case, but it was Lord Justice McDermott who carried the day by saying, 'The sentence cannot be impugned as being unduly lenient and was within the range of cases of diminished responsibility.' As a rider almost, he gave Susan Christie an additional four years, making it nine years in all that she had to serve. As she had already served part of her sentence, this did not leave her much more to serve, even including the four extra years that Lord Justice McDermott had given her.

THE PHOENIX TRUNK MURDERS

Probably two of the most macabre murders of all time were committed by Winnie Ruth Judd, who was born Winnie Ruth McKinnell on 29 January 1905, the daughter of a clergyman. Her childhood was an uneventful one, as is so often the case with murderers. She grew up to be a not unattractive copper-haired woman with big blue eyes, who worked as a student nurse at the Southern Indiana Hospital for the Insane in Evansville, Indiana. With hindsight, most people today would think that her place in the hospital would have been more appropriate as a patient, rather than a student nurse. During her time at the hospital she met and married William C. Judd, an elderly and wealthy doctor who was also on the staff.

When the doctor left the hospital to take up another appointment in Lafayette, Indiana, she went too and obtained a temporary job as a telephone operator just to be near him. It is not unusual for a man to fall for a woman much younger than himself, as was the case with the doctor. But for a woman to fall for a man much older than herself is often seen to be a different matter, and there is no doubt that Winnie Judd was besotted with the doctor, who was some twenty years her senior. An old hand when it came to courting younger women, the doctor had already been married to seventeen-year-old Lillian Colwell, who had died from natural causes only a month after they were married.

Pleased with himself at having found a new young woman, the doctor had vigorously courted her with the result that they were married in April 1924.

All went well with the marriage until Winnie became pregnant and then had to have her pregnancy terminated because of ill health.

The doctor and his wife later moved to Phoenix, Arizona, where Winnie made friends with Agnes Anne LeRoi, aged thirty, and Helvig Samuelson, aged twenty-two, a school teacher who seemed to be liked by everyone.

In August 1931, Mrs Judd's husband became restless again and he went off to Los Angeles, California, in search of yet another job. When this happened, Mrs Judd moved in with the two girls, and the three of them got on extremely well together, until Winnie suddenly moved out of the apartment and took another at 1130 East Brill Street, making the excuse that it was nearer to her work at the Grunow Clinic, where she was now employed.

Dr Judd seems to have had considerable difficulty in finding himself a new job judging from the inordinate length of time he was away. Perhaps the truth of the matter was that he was becoming bored with Winnie's company, a person who could be overbearing in her manner to most people. Or perhaps he merely wanted some time to himself. Whatever the reason, he was still not back by the middle of October that year.

On 17 October, Winnie Judd phoned in to the office from her flat and informed them that she would be a little late. There was also a second call that morning from someone purporting to be Mrs LeRoi, saying that Mrs Judd would not be in that day. The person who received the call was convinced the caller was actually Mrs Judd pretending to be Mrs LeRoi. Later that morning Winnie Judd did turn up at her office, highly nervous. It was not surprising that she was.

Earlier, after a late-night party with her two friends, Helvig Samuelson and Anne LeRoi, she had quarrelled with them, accusing them of interfering in her love life. Not unnaturally, her two friends had burst out laughing at the thought, at which point she had produced a small revolver and shot them both dead.

Considering that her friends had been alive one minute and dead the next, lying at her feet, Winnie Judd behaved with remarkable calmness. First she called the Lightning Delivery Co. and asked them to collect two trunks which she made ready for collection. While she was waiting for them she managed to cram the bodies of the dead girls into them, but not before she had found it necessary to saw Helvig Samuelson into several pieces. This must have been extremely difficult for her as she had previously fired a bullet into her own hand. Winnie wanted to claim that she had acted in self-defence when one of the girls had tried to kill her. After she had sawn Helvig Samuelson into pieces which could be easily fitted into one of the trunks, she then crammed Mrs LeRoi into the larger of the two trunks and sat down to wait for the delivery company to collect them.

The trunks were duly collected and stacked on a rack to await delivery to California. Soon the two trunks started giving off a vile smell, not unlike rotting meat. In addition, one of the trunks was leaking so badly that the floor of the baggage room became covered with a layer of an unpleasant-smelling glutinous substance. The baggage clerk was sure he had caught the hunter who was shipping venison illegally from Arizona to California.

Winnie herself duly arrived in California and went to the baggage room to claim the trunks, but the baggage agent had been summoned on account of the suspicious smell, and he told her that he must examine the contents of the two offending trunks.

'My brother has the keys,' she told him calmly. 'I'll have to get them from him.'

'I hope he's not going to be long,' the man said. 'The stuff in the trunks is getting pretty high.'

It was at this point that Jason McKinnell, Winnie's brother, turned up in answer to a call that she had put through asking him for his help in removing the trunks.

'I haven't got any keys,' McKinnell told the baggage agent testily, wondering why exactly he had been called to the baggage office.

'I suppose I shall have to phone my husband,' Winnie said. 'He must have them. I'll have to get him to bring them down here.'

She turned away quickly and went out of the baggage office with her brother, who was becoming more and more puzzled. Convinced that something was wrong, the baggage agent immediately phoned the police.

In due course two detectives arrived and proceeded to prise open the trunks. After some difficulty, one of the detectives, a man named Frank Ryan, finally managed to open his. He bent over and pulled aside a number of documents, only to stop abruptly.

'Jesus!' he said hoarsely. 'This is not venison meat. It's bits of a human body!'

He then put his hand into the trunk again, and bit by bit, produced a leg severed at the knee, then the upper part of a torso, followed by various other bits of a body. By the time he had finished he was looking distinctly green about the gills, and it was only by a supreme effort he was able to prevent himself from being violently sick.

The detectives were just beginning to recover from the effects of their grisly discovery when they had a surprise visit from the woman in charge of the train station's rest room. She was carrying with her a suitcase which contained the missing pieces of Helvig Samuelson's body, which Winnie had been unable to force into either of the trunks.

The police wasted no time in getting down to making their inquiries about Winnie Judd and her brother. They had no difficulty in tracking down Jason McKinnell, who was outside Dr Judd's house holding a conversation with him. McKinnell seemed only too anxious to talk. He told them that when he had met Winnie at the station she had told him she had been shot in the hand, and that there were two trunks he must help her to get. 'We must take them to the beach and throw them into the ocean,' she had said.

'What the hell is in the trunks?' he had asked her, and she finally admitted that they contained two bodies.

151

'Don't ask me any more. Anyway, the least you know about it, the better,' she told him.

'I gave her a $5 bill and that was the last I saw of her,' McKinnell added.

As for Judd, he had now become thoroughly confused by the course of events, and was to remain so until his death a couple of years later.

Winnie Judd seemed to have completely vanished and there was still no sign of her when her husband began putting advertisements in the newspapers asking her to give herself up. In the beginning he got no answer, and the police became convinced she had drowned herself and that in due course her body would be washed up on the beach.

During all this time Winnie had been holed up in a vacant cottage in the grounds of La Vina Sanatorium, only some twenty miles away. From the cottage she had made daily excursions into the sanatorium, from where she had filched a regular supply of food from the kitchens.

Suddenly, another advertisement appeared, with Dr Judd imploring her to give herself up, and stating that he had hired two attorneys who would do their utmost to save her from the death sentence. This time the plea had its desired effect. One of the attorneys, a man named Cantillon, for whom she asked on the phone, spoke to her. 'This is Mrs Judd,' she said. 'Can you please put me in touch with my husband?'

The upshot of this telephone conversation was that a meeting was arranged between Winnie and Dr Judd, who was accompanied by Mr Cantillon and the police, in, of all places, the funeral parlour of Alvarez and Moore, among the corpses. Dr Judd and Mr Cantillon were shown into an

Left: Thomas Allaway, mouth half open as usual, murdered prospective cook Irene Wilkins. (*Syndication International*)

Below: Allaway's demeanour in court did little to help his cause. (*Syndication International*)

The police search Drumkeeragh Forest Park, the scene of the murder of Penny McAllister. (*Pacemaker Press*)

Norma and Desmond Squire, the parents of Penny McAllister, leave Downpatrick Court during the trial of Susan Christie. (*Pacemaker Press*)

Winnie Judd, who shot two of her friends and then bundled their bodies into two trunks. (*Associated Press*)

Above: Elizabeth Maud Jones, the striptease artist who was lured by the glamour of Hollywood gangster films into committing murder herself. (*Syndication International*)

Above right: Karl Gustav Hulten, the Chicago GI who shot taxi driver George Heath. (*Associated Press*)

Right: Violet Hodge, who nearly died at the hands of Jones and Hulten but lived to tell her tale at their trial. (*Syndication International*)

upstairs room, where Winnie Judd lay on a bed, looking very poorly. Although there had been an attempt to dress her hand, it was badly infected. The police were also in attendance, and for their benefit she launched into a long rambling story of how she had come to shoot her two friends.

'I met Mrs LeRoi shortly after I arrived in Phoenix,' she told them. 'We became firm friends, and eventually she invited me to her home, where I met her friend Helvig. She was a beautiful girl and she loved all men. She loved a good time. I got to know them very well, and eventually I moved in with both of them. We were all very happy together.'

She paused, as if to collect her thoughts. 'During the months I was in Phoenix I had made friends with a millionaire lumberman named Jack. He was a good man and a true friend to me. I then introduced Mrs LeRoi to him and they seemed to get along well enough. After I moved in with them we held a number of parties, and Jack would come along with some of his men friends.'

Winnie Judd talked in a low, steady voice that betrayed no trace of emotion as she continued with her recital. 'Jack was very kind to me and Anne LeRoi began to resent it. Finally, I had to move to an apartment of my own, and Anne became very cool towards me. There was another girl at the clinic where I worked named Lucille and Jack found out that she was going on a hunting trip into the White Mountains, and he thought it might be a good idea if they all went together. A dinner party was arranged for Lucille and Jack and it turned out to be a very successful evening. Anne LeRoi then invited me to dinner with her and Helvig, and although I was very busy that week at the clinic, I went along. By the time we had finished it was late and we were all very tired, so it was suggested I stay the night on the couch, to which I agreed.

'At breakfast the next morning, Anne suddenly began to upbraid me for inviting Jack to meet other women. Heated words were exchanged, and then suddenly, without warning Helvig sprang to her feet and ran into the bedroom, only to return with a pistol in her hand which she aimed at me. As she pulled the trigger I threw up my arms and the bullet struck me in the hand. I then threw my whole weight at Helvig, who fell to the floor. She fell behind the breakfast table, and I grabbed the revolver. I shot her twice in all. It was at this point that Anne ran at me with the ironing board, so I shot her too, purely as a matter of self-defence.'

She sank back against the pillows, seemingly quite exhausted by her recital of what had happened. As well she might have been, as the whole thing was a pack of lies from start to finish. Certainly, as a story it sounded plausible enough. If she managed to convince everyone that it was true, the worst sentence she could get was the statutory one for a verdict of manslaughter.

'Before you take her in,' Dr Judd said, 'I'll take her down to the hospital and get that hand of hers dressed.'

She was taken to the George Street Receiving Hospital, where a twenty-five calibre bullet was removed from between her middle and index fingers. While this was going on, a crowd of some five hundred people gathered outside the hospital trying to catch a glimpse of Winnie Judd, such was the interest in her case.

She continued to claim that she had killed the two

women in self-defence. She repeated her story at her trial which began on 19 January 1932, but the jury were unconvinced. Winnie's mother and other members of the family came forward at the trial to state that there had been insanity in the family for generations. To add support to their contention, Winnie made a dramatic show of being insane. She constantly tore at her clothing and pulled violently at her hair, and generally behaved like a madwoman. On one occasion when the trial was nearing its end, still pursuing her attempts to convince the jury of her insanity, Winnie called out hysterically to her husband in a voice that could be heard by everyone in the courtroom . . . 'Let me throw myself out of the window!' She continued to rave until she had to be removed from the court. It was all to no avail as she was found guilty and sentenced to death by hanging in the Arizona State Prison in Florence.

Throughout the early days following her sentence, her father, the Reverend McKinnell, was at her side for much of the time, and there were to be many stays of execution. Her antics continued to occupy the headlines until, at last, the State of Arizona gave in and judged her to be insane. In 1933 she was transferred to the Arizona Hospital for the Insane. Her death sentence was eventually commuted to life imprisonment, but it was far from being the end of her story.

Once she had adjusted to the strict routine of the hospital she began taking care of the very ill herself, applying her nursing training to the welfare of the patients. Once again, this should have been the end of her story. Instead, for the next fifty years she continued to occupy the headlines. Whenever the press became short of material they knew they could always fall back on the escapades of Winnie Judd.

After she had tried to escape several times there was a lull in her activities until October 1939, when she calmly walked out of the asylum almost under the very eyes of her attendants. This time she left a note for the Governor of Arizona, saying she was off to see her ailing father and would be back in due course. A few days later she duly reported back to the asylum and carried on as before, as though nothing had happened. A month later she was at it again, leaving the institution with such ease that the asylum came under attack for allowing her to escape.

Over the next twenty-four years she made no fewer than four more escapes, by which time she had become a beloved figure to most of the inmates around her.

Then on 8 October 1962, she escaped yet again and completely disappeared for six and a half years, by which time she had changed her name to Susan Leigh Clark and got herself a job with a wealthy family named Blemer. Eventually she was recognised on the street in 1969 and promptly arrested. She got a lawyer named Melvin Belli to fight the extradition order to Arizona, but the matter was finally settled by the then Governor of California, Ronald Reagan.

On 2 December 1971, her life sentence was commuted, and she was released on the condition she lived out the rest of her life in California.

This time she went back to her former job in the Blemer home until Mrs Blemer died in 1983. When the other relatives threw her out, she sued the estate for a not inconsiderable amount, claiming that since her parole in

1971 the family had kept her as a virtual indentured servant. To her surprise, and to the horror of the remaining members of the Blemer family, she was awarded a $225,000 settlement, plus $1,250 a month for life.

THE MURDERER WHO WOULD BE A WRITER

Strood, in Kent, is a rather dreary little Medway town where nothing ever seems to happen, and is notable only for once being an area where the novelist Charles Dickens spent much of his life, and where he set *The Pickwick Papers* in the various inns around the area.

On 9 October 1942, the stillness of the chill evening air was suddenly broken by the sound of violent screaming.

On hearing the screams, a gentleman who lived in a nearby house called Valhalla, hurried out to see where all the noise was coming from. Turning a bend in the road, he was horrified to see a local woman he knew as Mrs Symes, lying in the road, bleeding from a wound in the neck. An overturned pushcart nearby contained her little boy of four who was kicking his legs helplessly, and who was obviously very frightened.

By the time he had picked up the child, gone to telephone for a doctor, and afterwards the police, and then returned to the injured woman, she had already died.

As it was now after ten o'clock at night, the police did not seriously begin their inquiries until the next morning. They were, however, able to establish that the victim was a married woman in her mid-thirties, who had been married to Alfred Symes, a joiner, who was at present doing some part-time work at one of the local munitions factories. In addition to their four-year-old son, the family had been looking forward to the arrival of another child in five months' time. They lived in a pleasant enough house in Strood which they had named Thames Mount, and which suited them very well as it was near her aged parents' house in Dickens Terrace.

On that evening Mrs Symes had set off to see them, her regular practice every Friday. After she had accompanied her parents to the Wainscott Workers' Institute, where her mother and father socialised with the neighbours, she had waved them goodbye, and that was the last they or anyone else had seen of her.

Early the next morning the police began their inquiries, and almost from the start they were able to home in on a man named Buckfield, often nicknamed 'Smiler' for obvious reasons. He originally came from Houghton near Manchester, where he had lived with his wife and three children until he joined up. He was posted to Strood, and then deserted soon after. While on the run he had managed to support himself by making a living of sorts as a casual labourer and by fruit picking.

Once they had begun to explore the area, the police had little trouble in finding Buckfield, who was well known to many of the local people, and seemed a likely suspect from the beginning as they were sure he was a deserter. After tracking him down, they asked him if he would care to give them an outline of his movements on the night of the murder.

'I would be glad to,' Buckfield told them. 'After I left work that evening I had some tea opposite the Majestic. Then I had a game of billiards at the Seamen's Mission. Then I went to a public house called The Steam Engine. I stayed there until half past eight.'

Although his replies had been reasonable and could easily be checked, the Chief Constable was already sure they were on to something. Buckfield had been a little too ready with his responses, and far too on top of the situation for his liking. 'I'm very sorry,' he said courteously, 'I'm afraid I must keep you in for further questioning.'

By the following morning Buckfield became suspicious as to why the police were continuing to hold him. He had been under the impression that it was because he was a deserter, but now he began questioning their real reason. It then transpired that after the Chief Constable had asked him why he thought he was being held, Buckfield informed him that he had been 'held for questioning three times before'.

'What for?' asked the Chief Constable curiously.

'Murder,' said Buckfield, flashing him one of his famous smiles. Then, seeing the expression on the Chief Constable's face, added quickly: 'I was always innocent, of course.'

Mrs Symes' murder had been a mindless affair. Probably Buckfield had gone out that evening looking for a victim and she had been unlucky enough to be out at the time. We shall never know exactly what happened that night, except that she had been savagely attacked with a breadknife, which was later found by the police in an orchard, where it had been flung by the murderer immediately after the attack took place.

After several hours of extensive questioning, which had got the police nowhere, Buckfield was taken back to his cell. By this time the murder weapon had been discovered and sent to a pathologist, together with the uniform Buckfield had been wearing, and which showed a complete absence of any bloodstains. There were bloodstains on the knife, however, which were discussed at the trial. At the moment, however, the Chief Constable still had nothing which could justify bringing Buckfield to trial.

The maximum amount of time a prisoner is allowed to be held without charge is four days, and that period now being up, the police were forced to hand Buckfield over to the military authorities.

It was after he had been locked up that he handed over a bundle of handwritten pages of a detective story he had written. Entitled *The Mystery of Brompton Road*, by Gunner Buckfield, it was an illiterate piece of work which made it all too clear that Buckfield was no writer. It was this story, more than anything else, though, that led to his conviction. The narrative, written in the first person by Buckfield himself, contained so much information about the crime that it could only have been written by the murderer.

The Chief Constable mulled over the situation and finally decided that even with the detective story, he did not have enough evidence, after all, to establish the guilt of the prisoner. Another four weeks were to pass before he was sure enough of himself to bring a charge of murder against Buckfield.

In the meantime, the intervening weeks had not been without incident. One evening, a police inspector had visited the military prison where Buckfield was being held, and confronted him with the statement that a soldier named O'Hara had come forward to say that he had seen Buckfield with a similar knife to the one used in the murder.

On being told this, Buckfield had done that very rare thing for him. He had lost his temper. 'It's a confernal [*sic*] lie,' he shouted. 'Let me face him and have it out!'

Needless to say, Buckfield's wish was not granted and his trial began on 20 January 1943, before Mr Justice Hallett, with Mr L. A. Byrne appearing on behalf of the prosecution, and Mr Hector Hughes, KC, acting for the defence.

Very early on in the proceedings, Mr Justice Hallett made a sarcastic reference to Buckfield's short story. 'A very disastrous thing, wasn't it,' the judge remarked, 'that you should have, out of all the tens of thousands of roads in London, selected the one road that happened to have the same name as the one where the murder happened!'

'Well, it seems that way, my Lord, yes,' said Buckfield quietly.

During the whole trial, Buckfield remained remarkably calm, keeping that fixed smile on his face throughout. It was only when Sir Bernard Spilsbury, the famous pathologist, came forward to give evidence, that he took any interest in what was being said. Up to then he had behaved like a man who was so convinced of his innocence, that he was sure it would only be a matter of time before he was released.

'What was the cause of death of Mrs Symes?' Sir Bernard was asked.

'A haemorrhage resulting from a stab wound in the front of the neck,' Sir Bernard said briefly.

'Could that wound, in your opinion, have been self-inflicted?' he was asked by Mr Byrne.

'No.'

Sir Bernard Spilsbury was then shown the murder weapon. 'Look at this knife. This is exhibit A. In your opinion, could the wound have been caused by this knife?'

Sir Bernard nodded. 'It is possible, though it would have required a great deal of violence with this knife to produce that injury.'

Having established that the knife could indeed have been used as the murder weapon, Mr Byrne and Sir Bernard launched into a discussion as to how the blood might have gushed from the victim. This puzzled the jurors, as it seemed to have no bearing on the case.

This wandering off the subject occurred a number of times during the trial, until Mr Justice Hallett was constrained to mention it to Mr Hughes, acting for the defence.

During Mr Hughes' examination of the husband of the dead woman, he was asked, 'So far as you know, did anything happen to her while she was going from your house to her parents?'

'Nothing happened to her,' Mr Symes replied.

'Counsel for the defence is asking you in great detail as to which way she went, how she went from her house to her parents,' Mr Justice Hallett ventured. 'And the jury will be told that the evidence will show that she was murdered coming from her parents' house three hours later.'

'What I want to find out from you—' Mr Hughes began, addressing Mr Symes.

'Mr Hughes,' Mr Justice Hallett said sharply, 'I grudge no time, and the jury will grudge no time, but I really think some relevance should be observed. You see, here the jury are told they are inquiring into a case in which it is alleged that this woman, having left her parents at 9.23 p.m., was murdered on the way back to Thames Mount, and you have been asking this witness a whole series of questions as to what happened, which way his wife would go from Thames Mount to her sister's and subsequently to her parents' house, before anything happened to her. If it is relevant to the case you may ask the questions, but it is a little difficult to see at present how it can possibly be relevant to any case made by the defence.'

Realising that Mr Justice Hallett was distinctly displeased, Mr Hughes hastily tried to make amends, but only succeeded in making matters worse.

'We do seem, I respectfully agree,' admitted Mr Hughes, 'to have wandered into by-paths.'

Mr Justice Hallett fixed him with a frosty eye. 'I do not think you should use the word "we". The jury had not wandered there, and I am not conscious that I have.'

'What I want to find out is why it took the lady over an hour to get—'

Again Mr Justice Hallett interrupted him. 'Well, ask it, but do remember that there is a very serious matter here, and the more we concentrate on the very serious matters that are really relevant, the better the jury will be able to perform their responsible task. It does not help them to be wandering up the by-ways until they become exhausted before they come to the material part of their journey.'

After counsel for the defence and prosecution had made their respective cases to the jurors, Mr Justice Hallett spent the best part of two days on the summing up, which was a masterly breakdown of the evidence. 'Before you find the prisoner guilty, the Crown has to satisfy you by evidence of two things,' he said. 'In the first place they must satisfy you that the woman, Mrs Symes was murdered; they must exclude the possibility that she met her death by natural causes, or from disease or from accident. They must satisfy you that she was murdered, and she was murdered by this prisoner. As to the first point, whether she was murdered, you will probably have no doubt at all . . .' He then went through each statement that had been made, while making it clear at the same time that no motive had been established.

'It is not the business of the prosecution to show motive,' he said severely. 'The Crown, when they charge someone, are not bound to show motive . . .'

And so it went on, the careful building up of the evidence which eventually pointed the finger of guilt at Buckfield. Finally, Mr Justice Hallett made another reference to the damaging short story of Buckfield's. 'I have shown you nine references to Brompton Road in the document,' he said, and then went on to outline how it could only have been possible for the murderer himself to have known the facts contained in the story.

The jury retired to consider their verdict at 12.57 p.m. and returned at 2 o'clock with their verdict. It was the opinion of all of them that the prisoner was guilty. When it came to Mr Justice Hallett handing out the death sentence, Buckfield continued to smile, even when he heard the judge's solemn words. Two weeks later he was judged to be insane, was reprieved and then sent to spend the rest of his days in Broadmoor.

MURDER
WITHOUT MOTIVE

Kenneth Barlow was a man who had a lot going for him. He was thirty-eight, and was a quite personable-looking man with a reasonably well-paid job as a male nurse at the East Riding General Hospital in Huddersfield, where he was held in high regard by everyone on the staff. He was married to Elizabeth, an ex-nurse who had been his wife for less than a year and was already expecting a baby. Although she had first been against having the baby, Barlow had managed to persuade her that to bring the child into the world would only improve their relationship in the long term, and she had finally agreed to have it.

At the time, everything seemed rosy enough for them both, with Mrs Barlow taking an obvious pleasure in being with her husband whenever they were seen together.

It was at 11.30 p.m. on the evening of 3 May 1957 that a doctor was called out on an emergency to the residence of Mr and Mrs Barlow, who lived in Thornbury Crescent in the Yorkshire town of Bradford, where he was met on the doorstep by Mr Barlow, who seemed to be in a great state of agitation.

'Thank God, you've arrived, doctor,' he said, leading the

way up to the bathroom, where Mrs Barlow lay dead in an empty bath. 'I found her like this,' Barlow said as the doctor proceeded to examine her. 'I let the water out of the bath and then tried to revive her, but with no luck. I then went to the neighbours next door and asked them to phone for a doctor while I came back here and continued to try and revive her by artificial respiration.'

The doctor continued to examine the body with great care. He found no sign that Mrs Barlow had been knocked unconscious, so he then examined the body for puncture marks which would have told him that a hypodermic needle had been used. However, he did note that the pupils of her eyes were widely dilated.

It was only after he had examined the body for a second time that he found several minute puncture marks on the buttocks. 'I shall have to tell the police what my examination has revealed,' he said.

'Of course,' Barlow muttered.

At first the doctor had thought that Mrs Barlow had slipped, knocked herself unconscious and subsequently drowned. Instead, the discovery of the puncture marks had now made him decide that he might well be looking at a case of murder.

The doctor's suspicions were mild compared to those of the police when they visited the house immediately after the doctor had informed them that he had just finished examining the body of a female who had died in suspicious circumstances. They noticed that Mrs Barlow's pyjamas were soaked with perspiration, where they lay in the bedroom, and that Kenneth Barlow's, by contrast, were completely dry, which most certainly would not have been the case if he had tried to administer artificial respiration to Mrs Barlow. They had also come to the conclusion that the victim would have made some sort of splashing movements while she was drowning, and that this would have led to the bathroom floor being wet, when in fact it had been completely dry when the doctor had entered the bathroom.

When he had finished examining the body, Detective Chief Inspector Coffey, of the West Riding Forensic Science Laboratory at Harrogate, searched the house and found four hypodermic needles, which Barlow pointed out were there because they had been in use for various things prior to his wife's pregnancy. However, the doctor was of the opinion that because of the dilation of Mrs Barlow's pupils, a large injection of insulin had been given only hours before her death.

The police decided that Barlow had a case to answer, and they arrested him while they continued with their inquiries.

By the time the trial eventually began in the December of that year, no less than six months had passed since he had been arrested and the police had managed to acquire a great deal of damning evidence against him.

There was Harry Stork, a nursing orderly who had worked with Kenneth Barlow from Easter 1954 until Christmas 1955, and who distinctly recollected having a conversation with him at the Northfield Sanatorium in nearby Driffield, when Barlow had stated that one could commit the perfect murder by using insulin, which could never be traced because it soon dissolved in the bloodstream.

In addition, he had had a conversation with a nurse, Joan Waterhouse, who had also worked with Barlow, and who told the court that he had said to her: 'You could kill somebody with insulin as it can't be found very easily, unless you use a very large dose.'

As if this were not enough, the police produced another witness named Arthur Evans, a former patient of the Driffield Sanatorium who had been there at the same time as Barlow was on the staff. During that time he had had a conversation with him on the subject of insulin. In their talk together about it, Mr Evans definitely remembered him saying it was the quickest way out. Although all this was far from being conclusive that Barlow had murdered his wife, it did show that he was only too well aware of insulin as a potential murder weapon.

Nothing was clear cut in this trial. One of the problems never resolved was the complete lack of motive for the murder, something which the Solicitor General, Sir Harry Hylton-Foster, appearing for the prosecution, admitted to the court. What he did have, however, was a great deal of evidence to support his case.

Quickly, Sir Harry ran through the evidence leading up to Barlow's arrest. He then called Dr David E. Price, the Home Office pathologist who had examined the body, and he agreed that one of the injections had been given only a few hours before. Tests had been made on 1,020 mice which were injected with samples taken from the body, and elaborate experiments were carried out to make sure that it was insulin that had been used, the doctor informed the court.

It was now the turn of Mr Bernard Gillis, QC, to speak up on Barlow's behalf. 'Why should this man try and get rid of his beautiful wife?' he demanded. 'The jury has heard that nothing but affection and happiness had existed between them. He has told you that he was more in love with her when she died than when she first became his wife.'

Warming to his task, Mr Gillis continued, 'He has never injected insulin into her body, or taken any steps to bring about her death. There is not the slightest foundation for the allegation that he murdered her.'

To support his contention that Barlow had always been a loving husband, Mr Gillis called a Mrs Skinner, the next-door neighbour to the stand. 'Mrs Barlow was a charming woman,' she stated. 'The couple were very much in love. As for Mr Barlow, he was always a kind and devoted husband.'

All this may have been very much in Barlow's favour, and had even pointed to an early acquittal, but there were certain aspects of the case which were damaging to Barlow's claim that he was an innocent man.

There were the three phials that had gone missing from St Luke's General Hospital in Huddersfield, where he had been working at the time, and which had never been found. Sister Lodge, who had been in charge of the phials, also mentioned that Barlow had given a number of patients their nightly dose of insulin for their diabetes. As for the missing phials, they had never been found.

It was at about this point that the sympathy for Barlow began to evaporate, especially when he had reluctantly admitted to stealing the phials in order to give his wife injections of ergometrine in order to procure an abortion. He had obtained them at his wife's insistence when she had suddenly decided that she didn't want the child after all.

'Is there the possibility of you mistaking insulin for ergometrine?' Sir Harry asked.

'None whatsoever,' Barlow said firmly.

'Why did you not admit to stealing this drug from the beginning?' Sir Harry asked him.

'I thought it would detract from my reputation as a nurse,' he was told.

Concluding the case for the prosecution, Sir Harry Hylton-Foster said that it had been proved beyond all doubt that the cause of death had been from drowning.

In the middle of his closing speech there was an interruption from one of the jurors, who then went over and had a few worried words with Sir Harry, after which Barlow consulted his counsel and signed a paper agreeing to the case continuing, despite the fact that one of the jury had been taken ill. Sir Harry then rose to his feet again. 'If there is no objection, this case will be judged by eleven people instead of twelve. I regret to inform you that one of the jurors has fallen ill. I trust the defence has no objection.'

This having been agreed upon, the trial then proceeded.

It was now the turn of Mr Gillis QC to make the final plea for his client, which he did most ably. 'The standard of proof required by criminal law is much clearer and less ambiguous than the opinions put forward and sincerely held by scientists,' he began. 'There are several steps to the prosecution's case. That Barlow injected his wife with insulin, that the purpose of the injection was to render her comatose, and that while she was in this state she was open to persuasion, and that while she was in this state he did persuade her to take a bath and while she was in it she was likely to fall unconscious so that she had neither the will nor the energy to rouse herself from the water, and that submerged, she would remain long enough to drown and would not be awakened by the water.'

Sir Harry went on: 'I submit that the medical and scientific evidence did not go as far as to prove it was insulin that was found in Mrs Barlow's body. It was something that had the properties of insulin and behaved like that drug, but it has not been proved beyond all doubt that Barlow did in fact inject his wife with insulin.

'The suggestion has been made,' Mr Gillis continued, 'that this murder was planned before he had even married the deceased. One of the saddest aspects of this case are the lies he told about the ergometrine. In this he behaved very foolishly, and put himself by his own lies in terrible peril. That does not make him a murderer.'

After Mr Gillis had finished, Mr Justice Diplock, who had been judging the case, had this to say as part of his summing up: 'This is murder or nothing. If you are satisfied that the story of having given her artificial respiration cannot be true, you will ask yourself why he lied, and no doubt why he did not give her artificial respiration. Was it because he intended her to die?' He went on in this vein at some length, and by the time he had finished there was little doubt as to where his sympathies lay. He ended his summing up by saying: 'You must ask yourself whether an overdose was injected by the accused, and if the answer is yes, did he intend to kill? If the answer is again yes, you must bring in a verdict of guilty.'

The jurors, who seemed to have taken against Barlow, left the court grim-faced, to consider their verdict. They were out for ninety minutes and they returned with a verdict of guilty. Kenneth Barlow was sent down for life.

He was released from prison in 1984, after having served twenty-six years behind bars. He came out in the same way as he had gone in, still protesting his innocence.

In the face of the evidence it is still possible to maintain that Barlow was innocent and even support the claim with much of the evidence. But before you come down too strongly on his behalf, it is worth mentioning that he had been married before and that his wife had died suddenly at the age of thirty-three, the same year that he remarried. A post-mortem had been carried out, when the doctors had been unable to state the cause of death, but had all agreed that death had been from natural causes.

Is it not possible that Barlow had got rid of his first wife by some mysterious means, and having got away with it the first time, had then proceeded to rid himself of his second wife, if only for the reason that he had suddenly tired of her? His relationship with the second wife had therefore been nothing but a sham which had been carefully sustained over the months.

If this is anything approaching the truth, it is hardly surprising that Justice Diplock in his summing up had referred to the murder as being a cold, cruel and premeditated one.

THE
CLEFT-CHIN MURDER

Elizabeth Maud Jones was an eighteen-year-old striptease artiste who performed under the professional name of Georgina Grayson, and in the normal course of events she probably would have ended up as yet another tired and overblown stripper who might have been just lucky enough to have got the odd engagement at one of the sleazy Soho nightclubs, where the strippers operated under dim lights, which helped to conceal the advancing age of so many of them.

The trouble with Elizabeth was that she was obsessed with the cinema to an unhealthy degree, and in particular with actors like Humphrey Bogart, Edward G. Robinson and James Cagney, who all specialised in playing gangsters. It was actors like these that she particularly admired, and who occupied her attention to the exclusion of almost everything else.

In time she would probably have grown out of her addiction to the exploits of these mythical gangsters, but unfortunately, she happened to fall in with Private Karl Gustav Hulten, aged twenty-two, who had recently deserted from the American forces.

Hulten was Swedish by birth, but American by upbringing, and had been trained as a paratrooper in the United States, eventually being sent to England to take part in the liberation of Europe. Upon his arrival in England he had deserted. Obtaining an officer's uniform, he then went around posing as Lieutenant Ricky Allen.

The early 1940s saw the cult of the gangster movie, with the stars playing characters who went to the gas chamber with a defiant grin, or were mown down in a hail of bullets in the last reel. Like Elizabeth Jones, Hulten was also attracted to the image of the gangster in the movies, with the result that he was in the habit of assuming the entirely fictitious role of Chicago Joe, who was supposed to control his own gang in London.

Unfortunately, Elizabeth was violently attracted to the sort of image Hulten was so fond of assuming. They met in a cafe, where they were introduced to each other by a mutual friend, a coach trimmer named Len Bexley, and it was therefore not even the beginning of a grand passion between them, but rather the excitement of being with what Elizabeth took to be a real, live hoodlum, while Hulten revelled in playing that part for her benefit.

Their doom-laden association started off with exchanging greetings which were notable only by their ordinariness. Certainly nothing was said that would have given anyone an inkling that they were about to embark on something that was soon to destroy them both and bring them to the Old Bailey on a charge of murder.

'Pleased to meet you, I'm sure,' she said as they shook hands.

178

'Hiya doing, babe?' Hulten said laconically.

'I'm all right.'

Hulten looked her up and down. 'Tell you something. Why don't you and me take a little ride tonight?'

'Why not?' said Elizabeth.

'Pick you up at 11.30 then, outside the Broadway cinema.'

She turned up that evening as they had arranged, but when he failed to put in an appearance, she walked from the Broadway cinema down the street and headed for home. She had only gone a little way when Hulten pulled up beside her in a truck.

'What would you like to do, babe?' Hulten asked her after she had climbed in beside him. He looked her straight in the eye. 'By the way, this truck is stolen. Thought you'd like to know.'

There was something about his manner which made her realise instinctively that they were about to do something really dangerous. Her heart began to beat faster. 'I'd like to do something exciting,' she breathed. 'I could be your gun moll.'

Hulten stopped the truck and looked at her in silence for several moments. Then, without a word, he started it up again.

For the next four nights they became vicious gangsters. Their method of operation was very simple and robbery was the main object of the exercise. First they would offer a lift to some unsuspecting person, who was then driven to a deserted spot where Elizabeth and Hulten would rob them before speeding away in the truck.

After they had done this successfully on several

occasions, Elizabeth said suddenly, 'I'm getting bored with this. Why don't we kill someone?'

'What – just for the fun of it, you mean?'

'Sure. Why not?'

Hulten shrugged. 'If that's what you want.'

Their opportunity for murder came on the night they were driving along the Edgware Road. Seeing a girl carrying a heavy suitcase Hulten pulled in beside her.

'Can we give you a lift somewhere?'

'That's very kind of you,' the young woman said breathlessly. 'As it happens, I'm going to Paddington Station to catch a train to Bristol.'

'Tell you what,' Hulten said. 'We're going down as far as Reading. Why don't we give you a lift as far as there? You'll save a mint of money that way.'

'It's very kind of you,' she said, as he took the suitcase from her.

When they had almost gone through Runnymede Park and were heading towards Windsor, Hulten suddenly stopped the truck. 'Sorry,' he said, 'I'm afraid we've got a flat tyre. You might as well take the opportunity to stretch your legs.'

The two women got out, and while the girl they had picked up was lighting a cigarette, Hulten hit her over the head with an iron bar. She screamed, but did not fall, and he then forced her to the ground. 'Go through her pockets,' he ordered Elizabeth breathlessly.

By then the girl had ceased struggling and Jones was able to search her handbag, in which she found exactly five pounds. Hulten then picked the girl up by the shoulders. 'Give me a hand here,' he said. 'We'll dump her in that stream over there.' Jones picked up the girl's feet, and the two of them carried her inert body over to the stream, where they dumped her. Unfortunately for them, her body was not properly submerged and she lived to tell the nightmare incident in court.

It should have been a nerve-shattering experience for both of them, especially as they were under the impression that they had killed their passenger. In actual fact, Hulten was so unmoved by it all that he was able to go to the cinema that evening with another girlfriend. As for Elizabeth Jones, she was so busy gloating over what they had done it is highly doubtful that she had the slightest twinge of conscience about what had happened.

It was inevitable that having seemingly got away with it so easily the first time they should wish to do it again as soon as possible. At the next opportunity Hulten picked up Elizabeth from her lodgings and together they set off. Although neither of them spoke it was clear in both their minds what they intended to do. On foot they went along the Hammersmith Road, where they stood in a doorway until they saw a cab come along. It turned out to be a private hire car which they hailed.

'You free?' Hulten enquired.

'That's right. Where do you want to go?'

Hulten said the first place that came to his mind, which was some way out of central London. 'We want the Chiswick roundabout at the end of the Great West Road.'

'That'll cost you ten shillings.'

Although he had hardly any money in his pocket and the fare was dear for those days, Hulten didn't argue. He clambered into the car and Elizabeth got in beside him.

During the journey they hardly bothered to exchange a couple of sentences with the driver. Instead, Hulten surreptitiously took out a revolver which he cradled in his lap all the way to the Great West Road. Seeing the revolver, Elizabeth started to say something, but Hulten silenced her with a warning glance. Once they were past the Chiswick roundabout, he spoke quietly to the driver.

'Okay. Stop the car. We'll get out here.'

The driver pulled in at the kerb and as he did so Hulten shot him in the back. Moaning, the driver slumped in his seat. 'Shut up, or I'll give you another of the same,' Hulten snarled. The driver had fallen to the left of the wheel and Hulten then got into the driver's seat himself and drove towards Staines.

'Go through his pockets and see what you can find,' he said to Elizabeth.

'Is he dead yet?' she whispered.

'Never mind if he is or not,' Hulten said impatiently. 'Just look in his pockets like I told you.'

Elizabeth leaned over and did as she was bid, emptying all of his pockets and handing over the contents to Hulten, including his cheque book and identity card which he threw contemptuously out of the car window.

Hulten pocketed all his loose change and his wristwatch, fountain pen and pencil which he later sold for paltry amounts. Their unfortunate victim then began to haemorrhage and Hulten swore as he watched the blood ebbing from his mouth as he died. 'Hell – let's get him out of here,' he said, edging the dying man out of the car and into a nearby ditch.

Their victim was a thirty-five-year-old taxi driver named

George Heath, who had a distinctive cleft chin, which led to him being referred to as 'the man with the cleft chin' and the case being called 'The Cleft-Chin Murder' by the popular press.

'Shouldn't you finish him off?' Elizabeth Jones whispered.

'Why waste a bullet on him when he's going to die in a few minutes?' Hulten said brutally as they drove off.

Incredibly, when Hulten left Elizabeth Jones that night he went straight on to his girlfriend, Joyce. In his book it had been a trying night, and he was in need of some simple loving to help him unwind.

By this time Heath's body had been found, and the whole London police force was out looking for the stolen truck which Hulten had been using. As it happened, PC William Walters happened to see it standing outside the house where Joyce lived and he immediately telephoned Hammersmith police station. A posse of police, headed by an inspector, arrived post haste and took up positions outside the house to wait for the killer. Hulten emerged from the house at about nine o'clock, and as soon as he stepped outside PC Walters emerged from the shadows and seized him by the wrist. 'Is this your vehicle, sir?'

Taken by surprise, Hulten didn't answer him. PC Walters then immediately shouted to his colleagues who converged on their quarry. Before he knew quite what was happening he had been arrested and his pockets were searched, when the revolver was found. He was then taken to Hammersmith police station where he was charged with the murder of George Heath.

He was then handed over to Lt Robert Earl de Mott, a young American CID officer, who took him to HQ in

London for questioning. This was all part of the procedure that existed between the two governments which stipulated that no US soldier should be tried in an English court. Hulten admitted to de Mott that he was a deserter and that he had spent the night of the murder with Georgina Grayson. He then offered to show de Mott where she lived.

After he had done so, the British police entered the house where Elizabeth Jones had a room, where they found her in bed. She was promptly arrested and taken to Hammersmith police station, where she made a statement. At this time she was not even suspected of having been involved in the murder and she was allowed home.

She had managed to lie herself out of the situation so far, but being an extremely stupid young woman she promptly blurted something of the truth to a friend of hers when she met him in the street. He had commented on how tired she looked.

'I'm not surprised,' she said. 'I've been with the police for hours about this murder. You know the one. The case they've been calling "The Cleft-Chin Murder".' If she had left it at that, there is the faint possibility that she might still have got away with it. Instead, she added darkly, 'If you'd seen what was done last night, you wouldn't have been able to sleep at night.'

As it happened, the old friend she had just met was a War Reserve Constable named Henry Kimberley, who had been closely following the case in the newspapers. As he listened to her talking about it, Kimberley knew that something was wrong and he later telephoned Hammersmith police station.

In due course, Kimberley arrived at the house where

Elizabeth lived, accompanied by an Inspector Tansill, just as she was returning with her shopping.

'I'd like to ask you a few more questions about your movements last night,' he said politely.

'What did you bring him round here for?' she whispered fiercely to Kimberley as they went inside.

'I think you should just tell him the truth,' Kimberley whispered back at her.

'All right, I will,' she said surprisingly.

She then made a full confession. Why she should have done so at this stage is difficult to explain. Unless, of course, she had realised that this was the end of the road and that this was as good a time as any to blame Hulten for everything. This she promptly did, saying that he had threatened her and forced her to take part in the robbery much against her will. It was a poor excuse, but it was more than Hulten had to offer when it came to it. His defence was simply that he had been egged on by Elizabeth Jones to commit murder, which he had done merely to please her. 'If it hadn't been for that woman,' he said bitterly, 'I wouldn't be standing where I am today.'

Their trial began on 16 January 1945, the American government having waived its rights regarding American forces being tried in an English court. The trial lasted for six days, with the two prisoners blaming each other for what had happened. If there had been the slightest show of affection between them before, there was no sign of it now. Such was their violent hatred for each other that on several occasions the judge was moved to attempt to bring a more impersonal note to the proceedings.

None of it made any difference to the outcome of the

trial, and they were both found guilty and sentenced to death, but in Jones' case, with a strong recommendation for mercy.

When the death sentence was pronounced on them both, Elizabeth Jones was dragged from the courtroom screaming hysterically. 'It's lies – all lies. Why don't you tell the truth?'

Ignoring the uproar going on around him, Hulten stood in the dock, a calm, steady figure in uniform. When the time came for him to leave the courtroom, he stared steadily in front of him, hardly giving the jury a glance as he disappeared from sight.

Two days before she was due to be executed, Elizabeth Jones was reprieved. She did not see the outside world again until the January of 1954, by which time she was still only twenty-seven.

There was to be no reprieve for Karl Gustav Hulten, who was hanged at Pentonville Prison on 8 March 1945. He was just twenty-three.

A film version of this murder case was made in 1989 and was called *Chicago Joe and the Showgirl*, starring Kiefer Sutherland and Emily Lloyd as the murderous couple. Although the period detail and its background of wartime London are well enough done, it is basically a dull film in which no attempt is made to understand its characters who are presented as cardboard figures.

A LUST
FOR KILLING

Like so many serial killers, twenty-eight-year-old George
Cummins seems to have come from a good background,
with a father reputed to be a member of the House of
Lords. In common with so many killers of his kind,
Cummins was a rather good-looking man, though without
the style of someone like George Neville Heath. He had
joined the RAF at the outbreak of war and was an officer
cadet.

He first came to the attention of the public in February
1942 when he murdered and mutilated the body of Evelyn
Hamilton, who was found in an air-raid shelter in
Marylebone. Miss Hamilton was a highly respectable
woman of forty who had worked as a chemist's assistant in
Hornchurch, Essex, until she moved to London. Her body
had been found by an electrician, who had immediately
called in the police.

They arrived in due course, led by the famous Cherrill of
the Yard. Cherrill examined the body which he saw had
been badly mutilated, and apart from noticing that the
dead woman's scarf had been wound around her face like a
gag, and that her clothing had been disarranged, he

also saw some marks on the woman's neck. From their position he was able to deduce that the murderer was left-handed.

No sooner had the police come to terms with the fact that they had a particularly vicious murderer to deal with than Cummins struck again, this time killing Evelyn Oatley, whose throat was cut and whose body was found in a Soho apartment the very next morning.

As with the previous murder, the mutilation had been truly horrifying. Sir Bernard Spilsbury, the noted pathologist, whose last major case this was to be before his death in 1947, referred to her injuries as 'being quite dreadful' and gave the opinion that they had been carried out by a sex maniac.

It is worth mentioning at this point that Evelyn Oatley was a prostitute who operated under the professional name of Nina Ward. There is always the possibility that the customer might turn out to be a killer, as was the case with Cummins.

In the meantime, Cherrill had made some small progress: at the scene of the last crime detectives had found a fingerprint on the tin opener which had been used on Evelyn Oatley to carve up the lower portions of her body. Although Cherrill had quickly established that the fingerprint was not that of the victim, it could still have been made by anyone who was unknown to them, and not necessarily the murderer.

As it happened, this was a problem which was solved by the murderer himself, who was soon careless enough to leave proof of his identity at the scene of another of his crimes.

The police traced Cummins to his billet in St John's Wood, but it had taken them several days to find him, and by that time he had killed no fewer than two more prostitutes. His third victim was a forty-two-year-old woman named Mrs Lowe, whose mutilated body was not discovered until three days later. Cummins struck again on that same night, picking up a prostitute named Mrs Jouannet, this time making his escape by means of the fire exit.

During the time that Cummins was on a murder spree two more murders were put down to him, the nineteen-year-old Miss Mabel Church, whose body had been found mutilated in a bombed-out house in the Hampstead Road as early as the previous October, while another body had been found near Regent's Park which had also borne the hallmarks of his *modus operandi*. There might well have been more.

On Friday 14 February, Cummins picked up a Mrs Greta Heywood and took her for a drink at the famous Trocadero in Piccadilly. Afterwards they walked down the Haymarket together, with Cummins playing the role of gentleman up to the hilt, something which had already caused him to be called The Count by those who knew something of his social background. However, suddenly for some reason Mrs Heywood took a violent dislike to him, and now only wanted to go home.

Cummins' façade of respectability began to slip a little, and his manner changed. 'You must let me kiss you first,' he said thickly, edging her into a doorway and pushing her to the ground.

Under the weight of Cummins' body, Mrs Heywood's

legs gave way beneath her and she began screaming. This only seemed to inflame him the more, and he began to paw at her frantically as he tried to grip her throat. Realising that he was now completely out of control, Mrs Heywood continued to scream until his hands finally fastened around her neck, turning her screams into hideous gurgling noises as he tightened his grip.

Fortunately, an errand boy was in the vicinity, and ran towards the struggling pair. Seeing him approaching, Cummins fled into the night, leaving behind him his gas mask with his name, rank and number on it.

Only momentarily deterred by this setback, Cummins had recovered himself sufficiently within the next few hours to return to the West End of London for his next victim. Eventually he picked up a young prostitute named Mrs Mulcahy, and they went by taxi to her apartment in Southwick Street in the Paddington area.

It was a freezing cold night, and Mrs Mulcahy lit the gas fire after Cummins had handed her five pound notes. She then removed her clothing, but fortunately, as it happened, she kept her boots on. Cummins then proceeded to take off his own clothes and then suddenly caught her by the throat and began to squeeze.

It was at this point that Mrs Mulcahy was able to kick him hard on the shins, causing him to release his grip on her throat.

The pain in his legs where Mrs Mulcahy had kicked him seemed to have a peculiar effect on him. It was almost as if he had just emerged from some strange dream and was now returning to normality. Stammering out his apologies, he pressed another five pound notes into her hand. He then dressed himself as quickly as possible and left the flat without another word.

What is one to make of such strange behaviour? Perhaps the simple reason is that he panicked at the last moment, and remembering what had happened with Mrs Heywood, he was not anxious to risk being caught a second time.

Cummins' gas mask and the pound notes he had given Mrs Mulcahy enabled the police to trace him and Detective Inspector Greeno took him in for questioning. The Inspector (who has appeared before in the book – see Chapters 1 and 7) was faced with one problem which held up his inquiries: Cummins' name in the billet pass book showed that he was in at the time when the murders had taken place, and that he was therefore innocent.

It was not until Greeno found out that the pass book was regularly altered by the other airmen in the billet to cover one another's absences, that everything fell into place, and Cummins was formally charged and arrested in late February 1942.

It was still difficult to believe that this mild-mannered and quiet young man was guilty of the terrible crimes with which he was now charged. As Detective Inspector Robert Higgins wrote of him from the impressions he had got from the prisoner while ferrying him from the prison to the courtroom:

He chatted to me on everyday subjects as though he had not a care in the world. He seemed completely unaware of the seriousness of the charges against him. He had an irritating habit of wanting to shake hands each time we met.

Observed at close quarters he was not an obviously unpleasant person. He was inclined to be slow and steady in his speech. From the physical point of view he appeared quite normal, being well built and well proportioned, and would not have attracted special notice if put among a group of ordinary people. I did, however, take particular notice of his unusually large hands, which had been well kept. He was deceptively gentle in manner and quite good looking – a man not unattractive to women . . .

As you can see from this report on him, this man who had committed four murders in five days, and who was already being referred to by the police as another Jack the Ripper, was deemed to be a normal enough member of society. He came from a good family and had been well educated and had made a good marriage to the daughter of a theatrical producer who was to stand by him when he was arrested, refusing to accept the fact that he was a murderer. The one blot against his character was that he had never been able to hold down a job because he was constantly being dismissed for dishonesty.

By the time Cummins came up for trial at the Old Bailey in April 1942, Inspector Greeno had managed to amass a great deal of evidence against him that made it almost certain that the prisoner would receive the death sentence – including an initialled fountain pen that had been found in his tunic pocket and which had belonged to Mrs Jouannet, and two cigarette cases formerly the property of two of his victims and which Cummins had taken for his own use, plus a number of fingerprints, to say nothing of the gas mask

192

which Cummins had left behind when he had fled in a panic from the spot where he had tried to murder Mrs Heywood.

All this was conclusive evidence against Cummins, and the jury reacted accordingly by reaching a verdict in twenty-five minutes in which he was found guilty. Justice Asquith, who presided over the trial, sentenced Cummins to be hanged after what must have been one of the shortest trials on record.

Cummins was executed at Wandsworth Prison on 25 July 1942. His wife, in a touching display of misplaced loyalty, visited him every day, convinced to the last that the state was hanging an innocent man.

THE SUPER COP
WHO KILLED

Robert Erler was a Vietnam veteran with a good war reputation which he had acquired while serving as a Green Beret. Immediately after the war he had joined the Florida police, where he had rapidly earned among his colleagues the reputation of being a very good cop with a long string of successes to his name, many of them obtained because of his almost uncanny knack of being able to spot a 'wrong 'un' almost on sight. Time and time again he had made a successful arrest with nothing more to go on than his almost psychic powers, which led to the undoing of many a petty criminal.

With something like awe his colleagues would point to examples where even major criminals had been brought to book. They would talk about his incredible psychic powers, generally quoting the case when he had seen a seemingly deserted house which had been occupied by criminals fleeing from justice. On that occasion, Erler had entered the house, and after exchanging shots with those inside, he had arrested them and taken them, single-handed, to the local prison. It was little wonder that to his fellow officers on the force he was known as 'The Super Cop'.

Certainly to many women he must have seemed the catch of the year. He was still only thirty-four and was also conventionally good-looking, and it was obvious that he was strongly in line for promotion.

It was all too understandable that he should have been married for some time already. His wife had been a go-go dancer who had done her best to keep him poor by being a compulsive shopper. The Erlers produced a son, who stayed with his mother when the couple had ultimately separated. Now Erler lived on his own in a trailer home on the beach. He had found, a little too late, that he was by inclination a solitary person, and was certainly in no hurry to try marriage a second time.

Some people might think that Robert Erler was scarred from the start. He was one of a family of five boys and two girls, and they had all been brought up in Phoenix, Arizona. Their father was a strict disciplinarian and something of a religious nutter who made their lives unbearable, laying down a code of behaviour that was almost impossible for them to live up to.

Everything in his life went smoothly enough until the evening of 12 August 1974 when Erler returned from work and went for his customary stroll along the beach, where he nearly stumbled over the sleeping figures of Dorothy Clark and her twelve-year-old daughter.

He awakened them gently. 'I'm sorry,' he said, reasonably enough, 'but sleeping is not allowed on the beach.'

If he had not been in uniform, Dorothy might have been distinctly uneasy about him turning up like that, but she was reassured by the sight of his police clothes.

'I'm sorry, officer,' she apologised. 'We've hitchhiked all

the way from Georgia and we don't have any money to pay for accommodation for the night.'

'That's tough,' he said. He seemed to be lost in thought about something. 'Why don't you spend the night in my trailer?' he suggested suddenly. He grinned. 'My wife and our two-year-old son are there now, so you'll be quite safe.'

Mrs Clark gratefully accepted the offer and Erler led the way to his trailer which was no more than a dozen yards away. Once inside, she could see no sign of another woman or the young boy. 'I thought—' she began, and then lapsed into an uneasy silence before deciding to go.

'Let's get out of here,' she said, moving towards the door with her daughter, only to come to an abrupt halt by Erler, who was now standing stark naked in her path.

'Your mother is going to look after me,' he smirked at Marilyn. 'Let's you and I go for a little walk outside.' Still smiling, he picked up his revolver from the table. With his free hand he pulled on his trousers. 'I never go out without this,' he said. He gave the girl another encouraging smile. 'We won't be long.'

Twelve-year-old Marilyn was terrified, though Erler continued to smile at her. With that, Erler led her outside towards a small wooded area nearby, where he coolly shot her five times in the head, killing her instantly. He then hurried back to the trailer, only to find Mrs Clark had fled. Throwing on his shirt, he headed in the direction of the airport, guessing she had made for this destination. As luck would have it, he caught up with her and as she cowered away from him, he shot her five times. Incredibly, she survived to tell the tale.

What had turned this thirty-four-year-old man with an

excellent reputation for maintaining law and order, into a cold-hearted killer overnight?

After he had committed the crime, Erler was suddenly overcome with the realisation of what he had done, and in a sudden fit of remorse he telephoned in to his police station.

'I've just killed two people. A mother and her little girl,' he said, doing his best to disguise his voice. 'You'll find the bodies – one near the airport, the other on the beach. Please catch me.'

'Who's that speaking?' he was asked.

'Never you mind,' the policeman was told. With that Erler hung up.

He reported in to work the next morning, when he was informed that he was being assigned to a new murder case. He then had the ironic situation of being charged with hunting down a killer he knew to be himself.

Mrs Clark was still alive when the police found her, and she was rushed to hospital, where she gradually recovered from her wounds. As he was already regretting his initial confession, Erler kept well out of her way.

If great things were expected of Erler now that he was hunting for the killer of Mrs Clark's daughter, the police force were soon to be disappointed with his lack of success on the case.

In the evenings, after work, Erler went back to his trailer home, where he sat for hours brooding, or he went for solitary walks on the beach.

Then suddenly, without any warning, Erler turned in his badge, telling his superiors that his mother was dying of cancer in Phoenix. He had no sooner settled in there when he happened to turn on the TV set and learned to his horror that he had been identified as the killer of Dorothy Clark's daughter by a number of cops who had listened to Erler's anonymous phone call to the police station, and had recognised his voice.

It would have been easy for him to take off and make a new life for himself under a different name. Instead, he chose to give himself up to the police, who returned him to Florida to stand trial.

He was found guilty and sentenced to ninety-nine years in prison, with a further six months' hard labour.

This should have been the end of his story. But it was very far from being the end. The first six months in prison were undeniably hard for him, as being an ex-cop he was fair game for every prisoner who had a dislike of policemen, which was practically all of them. They were always picking fights with him while the warders deliberately looked the other way.

In all he spent four years in the state prison before he was transferred to the minimum security prison at Bell Grade. It was while he was there that he made a spectacular escape by swimming across a moat filled with man-eating alligators. It was an exploit that won him the reluctant respect of all the guards and prisoners. If he had remained in prison he would not have been eligible for parole for another thirty years.

He was on the run for months, working as a labourer under an assumed name in Mississippi, Illinois and Tennessee, before he was finally caught in the post office at Jackson, Mississippi, when he went there to collect a parcel, only to find several lawmen waiting for him. As he was being led away by the police, he broke free from them and leapt into his car, waiting outside with the engine ticking over.

The rest of it was like something from a movie, with the police firing wildly at Erler as he drove away. Bundling into their own car, they drove after him through the town in a frantic chase, which resembled something from a Keystone Cops film. Any comic elements to the situation ended abruptly when Erler drove into a swamp and tried to make his escape on foot, only to be brought down by a shotgun blast from a deputy sheriff.

Nowadays Robert Erler is a fully recovered man, back in prison, where he spends most of the time thumbing through his bible and generally leading the sort of life of which his father would have approved.

THE
HI-FI MURDERS

The early evening of 22 April 1974 was even warmer than
is usual at this time of year in Utah, when sixteen-year-
old Cortney Naisbitt made his way along the sidewalks
as he headed for the hi-fi shop in the small town of
Ogden.

Earlier that day he had had a flying lesson from his
friend, Wolfgang Lange, for whom he had a great deal of
admiration and respect. He had just finished his first solo
flight and was feeling pleased with himself, especially as he
had done well enough to win Wolfgang's grudging
approval. He was now looking forward to telling his mother
how well he had got on that day.

He must have been within a hundred yards or so of the hi-
fi shop when two black men entered it from the back door.
One of them was Dale Selby Pierre, who had been born in
Tobago, some twenty miles away from Trinidad, where he
had spent a relatively carefree childhood. He was dressed
in the uniform of a US airman, as was his companion, a
much taller man named William Andrews.

By the time that Cortney reached the shop, they had
caught and tied up everyone who had been inside when

they entered it. They were all hustled down into the basement, where everything of value was taken from them, with the exception of a few pieces of jewellery. They were ruthlessly bound hand and foot with speaker wire and subjected to the most appalling violence as they were being robbed. Upstairs, sounds of the hi-fi equipment being hauled away could be heard.

By now the unsuspecting Cortney had just entered the shop from the front entrance, where he found himself being confronted by a tall black man holding a gun to his face.

'Take another step and I'll put a bullet into you,' he was warned. Cortney was pushed down into the basement, where another man was waiting for him. Swiftly, he pulled Cortney's hands behind him and tied them together and then did the same with his feet. By the time he had finished, Cortney was trussed up like a chicken and completely unable to move. He was then placed in a corner of the room beside the bound figures of Stan Walker, the shop assistant, and Michelle Ansley, who had only recently been working there.

It was at this point that someone came in through the back door, which caused Stan Walker to groan in despair as soon as he saw who it was. 'Why did you have to come down here, Dad?'

Stan Walker's father had appeared at the bottom of the stairs. Almost in the same instant, Pierre pumped two warning shots into the wall.

'I'm just nineteen,' Michelle moaned from the floor. 'I don't want to die.'

Mr Walker Senior said calmly: 'Just take what you

want and go. I promise I won't try and identify you.'

Ignoring him, Andrews looked at the other. 'What do we do now?'

'What I said I'd do,' Pierre said softly. A peculiar smile hovered on his lips. 'Now we're going to have a little cocktail party.' He then produced a bottle from one pocket and a green plastic tumbler from the other, which he proceeded to fill with a thick blue liquid he then held out to Walker. 'Get it down then. It's quite harmless,' he lied. 'Nothing more than a mixture of vodka and a German drug which will put you out for a couple of hours.' Actually, what he had poured out was a large measure of Drano, a lethal caustic compound used for unblocking drains. He pushed the cup close to Mr Walker's face, who resolutely turned away from it.

'Man, this is a gun pointing at your head,' Andrews said, pointing his pistol at him. When Mr Walker still would not drink from the cup, Andrews spun him round roughly and proceeded to tie his wrists. Once this had been done, Walker was ordered to lie on the floor with the others.

It was at this point that Carol Naisbitt arrived at the hi-fi shop, after having stormed out of the house following a brief row she had had with her husband about their son.

'I just know that something has happened to Cortney,' she had said. 'Now you won't even help me to try and find him. For God's sake, the shop must have been closed for hours by now.'

'You're over-reacting,' her husband had said patiently. 'He's probably still at the airport, or has gone down to the library before coming home.'

Carol Naisbitt had left the house and driven down to the hi-fi shop, where she hoped to find her son. The store still seemed to be open, and she pushed open the door, when she found herself looking into the barrel of Andrews' pistol.

'What are you doing here?' he demanded. 'It's long past closing time.'

'Put that stupid pistol away,' she said impatiently. 'I'm looking for my son.' She was about to say something else, when she suddenly became aware of Pierre glowering at her from the shadows of the room. She then saw the gun in his hand and realised that there was something seriously wrong. The words died on her lips.

Taking the cup from Andrews' hand, Pierre advanced on her. 'Swallow that,' he ordered. 'And be quick about it. Like I told the others, it won't do you any harm.'

'I don't want it,' Carol said, turning her head away.

'Drink it and shut up,' Pierre snarled. He pressed the cup against her teeth, while he forced her head back. Carol swallowed the liquid down and immediately began to cough loudly, having great trouble breathing as the acid bit into her throat.

Pierre watched her coldly as she continued to cough and spew as she struggled to breathe. Then nodding his head decisively, he moved over to Cortney. 'Now you,' he said as he forced Cortney's lips open to receive the liquid. Cortney swallowed some of it and immediately began gagging and vomiting.

It was then Mr Walker's turn. He was given a cup of the nauseous liquid, which he only pretended to swallow,

204

letting the caustic solution drip on to the floor, burning the corner of his mouth as it trickled down his face.

Then, lastly, it was Stan's turn. He immediately began to gag as soon as the liquid reached his throat. Pierre tried to cover his mouth with masking tape, but the tape wouldn't hold.

It had been Pierre's intention to poison them all, but as the Drano only seemed to make them violently ill, he calmly and without haste shot Carol Naisbitt in the back of the head. He then did the same to Cortney, Stan Walker and his father. Andrews was obviously none too happy about what was going on, but he said nothing.

Almost as an afterthought, Pierre then went over to Michelle, and made her take off her clothes, which she did, calmly stacking them up in a corner of the room. He then led her into the next room, where he spent the best part of half an hour raping her. Then, when he had finished, he got to his feet and looked down at Michelle for a few seconds before shooting her in the back of the head. He then went back to the room where the captives lay. His arrival was acknowledged by Stan Walker's father who groaned out aloud when he entered. Pierre walked over to him and, by way of a little light relief, drove a ballpoint pen deep into his ear.

'Right, let's go,' Pierre said, kicking the ballpoint pen deeper into Mr Walker's ear as he made for the stairs.

This marked the end of one of the most horrifying murder episodes ever committed in the state of Utah. There was nothing in Dale Pierre's upbringing to explain why he had indulged in such sickening conduct. However, he tried to claim that he had sustained a severe head injury earlier in life while riding his motorbike but this was proved to have no basis in fact, though he did suffer a scalp wound at school necessitating several stitches, but it was superficial and did not result in any concussion. It is interesting to note, though, that there had been a history of violent crime in his family: his paternal uncle had been executed after hacking his own pregnant sister to death with a machete.

Pierre was simply an ice-cold psychopath who had already been in trouble with the police, mainly because of a series of car thefts which had been put down to him, as well as being the number one suspect for the murder of a black air force sergeant named Richard Jefferson, who had been found dead in his apartment, stabbed repeatedly in the face with a bayonet. So far, Pierre had got away with it. However, this time the nature of the brutal multiple murder made the police determined to catch the killers at all costs.

The police were on the scene quite quickly. At 10.30 that night, a police car containing a rookie cop named Kevin Youngberg, who was accompanied by officer Gale Bowcutt, an experienced policeman, noticed lights burning in the hi-fi shop as they drove by.

'I don't like the look of this,' Bowcutt said. 'Let's take a look-see.'

They both got out of the car and made their way towards the lighted window. Looking through it, they saw Mr Walker walking dazedly around the shop, a ballpoint pen sticking out of one of his ears. Without further ado, Bowcutt went inside, closely followed by his companion.

'What's going on here?' he demanded.

'They've all been shot,' Mr Walker said weakly. 'You'll find them all downstairs.'

The two police officers cautiously made their way down the stairs, which were in darkness. Youngberg flicked on his torch to light their path to the bottom. As they made their way down they were assailed by the stench of vomit. Blood and brains were spattered everywhere.

The rays of Youngberg's torch shone on to a horrifying scene of three bodies lying beside their own pools of blood and vomit.

'Christ!' Bowcutt breathed. 'Phone for an ambulance. Tell them there are people here who need attention. That's if they're not dead already.'

'Two negroes did this,' Mr Walker said. He still had made no attempt to remove the pen from his ear.

'You'd better sit down,' Bowcutt said. 'You don't look too good yourself.'

'First, I've got to try and save my son,' Walker said.

'Which is your son?' Youngberg asked.

Mr Walker immediately pointed a finger at Stan, and Youngberg went over and lit his face with the torch. 'I'm sorry,' he said, 'but your son is dead.' He then sank to his knees to have a closer look at Cortney. 'This one is alive,' he said. 'But I think he's been shot in the lungs.'

'Why not try and take off his shirt?' Bowcutt suggested. 'If the lungs have been exposed, you can cover them.'

Youngberg ripped the boy's shirt aside and examined the wound. 'His chest seems to have collapsed. At the moment he seems to be drowning in his own blood.' He turned the boy over carefully and positioned his head so that the blood could drain away.

Two ambulances had now arrived and stretchers were brought down. Two more police officers had also arrived, including Sergeant Dave White, who immediately took charge. 'Have you found a phone anywhere around here?' Bowcutt nodded. 'Then get anyone down here who might help,' White barked. 'And tell them to make it as fast as they can. This is a major homicide.'

It was then that Youngberg hurried past, suddenly retching as he headed for the exit.

'Take it easy,' White called out after him. 'I've been a police officer for seventeen years, and this is the most shocking thing I've ever seen. Take five minutes outside. Do you need a cigarette?'

Youngberg took the cigarette that White offered him, and then went outside. White went round all the bodies and briefly examined them. 'They all look dead to me,' he said, as the bodies were removed one by one and placed in the ambulances. 'There's no point in us hanging round here any longer,' he added. 'Let's move.'

First, he watched the two ambulance men guide Mr Walker to one of the ambulances. 'We're not going to forget tonight in a hurry,' he commented as he prepared to leave.

When the case broke it caused a major sensation in Utah, which had already seen more than its fair share of murders, including some of the work of the infamous Ted Bundy, the serial killer who had murdered forty people in the Salt Lake City area.

Fortunately, as it happened, the present case was very quickly solved. The first big breakthrough came the next day, and was made by two young boys who were in the habit of rummaging through the rubbish tip near the air force station for anything they might sell for a few dimes. On this day they had found not only the discarded bottles they were seeking, but a woman's handbag, a purse containing small change and a credit card, a fistful of other credit cards and a cheque book. There was also a man's wallet containing a driver's licence and a student pilot's card made out to Cortney Naisbitt as was the driver's licence. On their way home with their haul, they ran into eighteen-year-old Airman Paul Weldon, who lived at the base. As they knew him quite well, the two boys told him what they had found.

'What are you going to do with the credit cards?' Weldon asked them.

'We haven't decided yet,' said one of the boys. 'Want to see them?'

When Weldon nodded he was shown the credit cards and the wallet. Weldon examined them briefly. 'Tell you what,' he said. 'Why don't I phone the owners and tell them what's happened?'

After some argument, the two boys reluctantly agreed to hand over the wallet and the cards, and then resumed scouring other rubbish dumps for more bottles.

On his way back to base, Weldon stopped at a telephone box and called the number he found printed on the cheque book.

'Hello,' said Weldon easily. 'I've found a cheque book and a credit card belonging to a Miss Michelle Ansley. Could I speak to her please?'

'I'm afraid not,' the voice said tearfully. 'Michelle was murdered last night.'

The upshot of this brief conversation was that Weldon was asked to stay exactly where he was until a police car came to pick him up. Already beginning to wish that he hadn't interfered, Weldon waited by the telephone box until the officers came for him. At the police station he made a lengthy statement and was then driven back to the base.

On that same day the police received a telephone call from an airman on the base, telling them that he had overheard a conversation between two men whom he identified as Dale Pierre and William Andrews, in which it became obvious that they were the killers the detectives were looking for.

The police now had enough to arrest the two men on suspicion of murder. But being air force men there were certain complications to overcome before they could be arrested. Affidavits had to be made out to support the arrests and search warrants had to be prepared before they could even enter the rooms of the two men. These were duly prepared and signed by a civilian judge before they were finally allowed into the rooms under the supervision of a military escort.

Almost immediately a rental storage agreement was found in Dale Pierre's quarters. This led the police to a room full of the missing hi-fi equipment and Andrews and Pierre were arrested.

When the two men came up for trial, the prosecution had acquired a surprise star witness which should have made the case against them irrefutable. This was Mr Walker, whose wound in the back of the head had turned out to be only superficial, as was the damage to his ear. Apart from the fact that the Drano had burned deep into his skin and left him permanently scarred, he was relatively unmarked by his ordeal at the hands of the two killers, which, unfortunately, is more than can be said for young Cortney Naisbitt, who was still fighting for his life in hospital, and was to continue to do so for the best part of a year before he was discharged, maimed and crippled for the rest of his life. It says much for the devoted medical care he was shown by the staff at the hospital, to say nothing of the courage of young Cortney himself, that he was eased away from the brink of death and brought back to some sort of life again.

The trial lasted for exactly a month, and at the end of it, the judge handed down the death sentence to both murderers. What with Mr Walker's testimony and the verdict that followed, one would have thought that would have brought the case to an end with the two men being executed in due time. Not a bit of it.

In the state of Utah, a convicted murderer must have his case brought up for review no fewer than nine times when a stay of execution is sought. All this is hedged about with a process of law which allows all sorts of additional appeals to be made, with the result that in the case of Pierre, matters dragged on for another thirteen years before sentence of death was carried out.

During the thirteen years he was in prison Pierre spent his days studying books on finance, with a view to becoming a financial wizard, and his evenings quietly watching TV.

As for Andrews, he was to be on Death Row for eighteen years before being finally led out on 30 July 1992 and given a lethal injection. Cortney's brother, Brett, made the following comment on the legal delays:

. . . it just irritates people and angers people to think that this can happen and nothing ever gets done about it. Maybe this is the process of law, but I think they carry it too damn far.

THE KILLING
OF PC EDGAR

Woe betide anyone who is unwise enough to shoot a policeman. On the rare occasions when this has happened, we have seen the full weight of the force brought into play to catch the guilty party. The case of PC Gutteridge, who was killed by Browne and Kennedy in 1928, who were both found guilty and hanged for the crime, is a notable example.

Far less well known is the case of the shooting of Constable Nathaniel Edgar who was gunned down in cold blood on 13 February 1948 by Donald George Thomas, an army deserter who had been on the run for the preceding three months.

His background was revealing, inasmuch as it shows how a potentially good man can sometimes take the wrong turning and become nothing more than a petty criminal, despite showing so much promise at the outset.

Thomas was born on 16 July 1925, and went to school in Edmonton, where he stayed until he was fourteen. He was considered intellectually very bright, among the six best boys in the school, with a potentially brilliant future ahead of him. He had also been captain of the cricket eleven and

213

was a member of the Boys' Brigade.

When he started work, he seemed deliberately to choose the sort of jobs that would put no great strain on his capabilities, first as a telegraph messenger boy, and then as a junior clerk. By his sixteenth birthday, however, he had already been in trouble with the police, which eventually led to his being sent to an approved school during the time of the Second World War.

This seemed to have a salutary effect on him, for when he was released, he went to a technical school where he studied electrical engineering and mathematics. He was then called up for military service in January 1945, only to desert within fourteen days. He spent the next two years on the run, doing his best to support himself on the proceeds of his activities as a small-time criminal. Unfortunately, he found himself unable to make enough money to live on and lacking the know-how or the ability to get himself into the big time, he reluctantly gave himself up and had to serve 160 days in detention before he was allowed to continue his service in the army. After a very short time, Thomas decided that his first opinions about army life had been right after all, and soon after his release from detention camp, he deserted for the second time.

It was almost three months later that he was stopped in the street by Constable Edgar, dressed in plain clothes, who had been asked to stop any possible suspects who might have taken part in a series of robberies that had been carried out in the area. When PC Edgar asked him for his name and address, Thomas unthinkingly supplied him with the correct details, and he had faithfully recorded them in his notebook as being Donald Thomas of 247 Cambridge

214

Road, Enfield. PC Edgar had then asked for proof of his identity, and Thomas, in a moment of blind panic, had produced a gun and shot him down at close quarters. He had made no attempt to aim, with the result that the three bullets he fired entered the lower half of Edgar's body, two in his right groin and one in his thigh. He·was later found dying in a gateway in Wade's Road, in north London, and was rushed to hospital. Before PC Edgar died later that night he was able to name the killer.

The police had no difficulty in identifying Thomas as a deserter on the run, and they hurried to the address they had found in PC Edgar's notebook, but found he was not there.

Detectives then took the unusual step of issuing a statement in which they informed the public that the police urgently wished to interview Donald George Thomas, as it was thought that he might be able to help them with their inquiries. This brought an almost immediate response from a Mr Stanley Winkless, who informed the police that Thomas had been in the habit of visiting his house from time to time, until approximately three weeks ago, when he had run off with his wife.

A photograph of the erring wife was then put in all the national newspapers and drew forth an immediate response from a Mrs Smeed, who owned a boarding house in the Stockwell area. After she had told her husband that the photograph in the newspaper bore an uncanny likeness to the woman who was living in an upstairs room with a man, the police were at once told of the Smeeds' suspicions.

Soon afterwards, three policemen arrived and were later joined by an Inspector Moody from Brixton police station.

After a brief, whispered conversation among themselves, it was arranged that they should storm the room upstairs.

First, though, Mrs Smeed was to put them off guard by taking their breakfast upstairs. Mrs Smeed laid a tray for them and took it up, with the four policemen tiptoeing behind her.

'Your breakfast,' Mrs Smeed called out.

There was the sound of someone moving about on the other side of the door. Then a male voice called out, 'Okay,' at which point Mrs Smeed went downstairs, leaving the officers grouped tensely around the door, waiting to rush in at the first opportunity. Then the door opened slightly and they caught a glimpse of Thomas in his vest and pants peering cautiously outside. As soon as he saw the police he attempted to close the door, but before he could lock it, Inspector Moody and his officers burst into the room and leapt on Thomas, who had already reached the bed and was fumbling for something under the pillow. There was a short but violent struggle on the bed as Thomas tried to reach his gun. Finally, Inspector Moody was able to wrest the weapon away from him.

'Is this gun loaded?' the Inspector asked breathlessly.

'It's fully loaded with bullets,' Thomas said. He gave him an unpleasant grin. 'And they were all for you. You were lucky,' he added. 'I might just as well have been hung for a sheep as a lamb.'

'Take him away,' the Inspector said to the two policemen who now held Thomas firmly in their grip.

There was, of course, a woman in the bed, who was Mrs Winkless, and she was told to get dressed and was then taken in a separate car to Brixton police station.

216

US airmen William Andrews (left) and Dale Pierre were executed
for their barbaric murders in a hi-fi shop in Ogden, Utah.
(*Popperfoto*)

Left: Dr Keith Simpson, who identified the body of Rachel Dobkin and showed how she had been strangled. (*Topham Picture Source*)

Top: Polly Dubinski, who advised the police that her sister Rachel had gone missing. (*Popperfoto*)

Above: Auxiliary fireman Harry Dobkin, whose horrific crime was only uncovered by a bomb. (*Syndication International*)

Deck steward James Camb with his wife, who abandoned him when he was accused of murdering Gay Gibson. (*Popperfoto*)

Police experts examine the cabin porthole through which Gay Gibson's body was pushed. (*Topham Picture Source*)

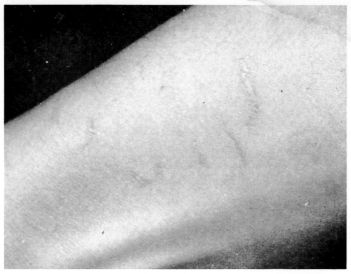

Above: The scratches on James Camb's body that formed part of the evidence which destroyed his story. (*Topham Picture Source*)

Below left: Gay Gibson, the troubled actress who met her untimely death onboard the *Durban Castle*. (*Topham Picture Source*)

Below right: Welsh Guardsman Michael Dowdall was described as 'a psychopath and a sexual pervert' during his trial. (*Syndication International*)

Later on that day the room was thoroughly searched and seventeen rounds of live ammunition were found, as well as a jemmy, a number of stolen identity cards and a rubber truncheon. There was also a well-thumbed copy of a book entitled *Shooting to Live with the One-hand Gun*, written by two Commandos, Captain W. E. Fairbairn and Captain E. C. Sykes. They also found Thomas's Luger automatic, which was later examined at the police station and found to contain eight rounds in the magazine and one in the breech. It showed more clearly than anything else that Thomas may have shot PC Edgar in a moment of panic, but had still planned to kill again if necessary. The bullets taken from Edgar's body were checked against Thomas's gun, and it was definitely established that they were fired from it. As if this were not evidence enough of his guilt, Mrs Winkless made a statement to the police in which she told them that Thomas had admitted to her that he had shot PC Edgar.

'I shot him twice in the legs,' he had confessed to her. 'I did not do it intentionally. But I had to get away from him somehow.'

All this by itself was enough for him to be remanded at Tottenham Magistrates' Court on 19 February. No charge was brought against the woman.

On 19 April he appeared at the Old Bailey on the charge of murdering PC Edgar. When asked to plead, he made a great show of springing smartly to attention and speaking out in a firm and resolute voice, 'Not guilty.'

His only defence was that the gun had gone off by accident, a statement which was refuted by Robert Churchill, the gunsmith expert. 'The gun was a thirty-year-old German service weapon,' he stated. 'It was a weapon

217

that needs a six-pound pressure on the trigger before it could be fired.'

In a final desperate attempt to save himself, Thomas put forward his version of what had happened. With the aid of an usher, Thomas tried to show the jury how PC Edgar had come to be mortally wounded. To illustrate the point, the usher held the muzzle of the gun in his hand, as if trying to push it down.

'That's when the first shot went off,' Thomas stated. 'I was trying to get away. The second shot went off behind him. The third shot was fired as he fell forward, his hand still on the muzzle.'

This line of defence had been suggested by Curtis-Bennett, and was one that did not seem to impress Mr Justice Hilbery, who pointed out that after the shooting, Thomas's gun was not only found to be fully loaded again, but had the safety catch off.

'At some time between the awful lesson that was supposed to have upset him so much that afterwards he did not know what he was doing, he had taken the trouble to see that the gun was fully loaded again,' commented the judge dryly. In his final summing up, Mr Justice Hilbery stated that if Thomas had pulled the trigger, intending to maim or kill PC Edgar, it was murder, but 'if the jury were satisfied that he did not pull the trigger intentionally, it was manslaughter'.

The jury took only fifty minutes to reach a verdict of murder. In view of the evidence against Thomas, it is a little surprising that they took as long.

Although he had been found guilty, Thomas could at least serve out his life sentence with the knowledge that he had been spared having to meet the hangman, as the murder had occurred shortly after the House of Commons had voted for a four-year suspension of the death penalty.

THE SECRET OF
MOAT HOUSE FARM

Samuel Herbert Dougal had served with the army for twenty-one years, but whether or not he had the right to call himself 'Captain', as was his wont when he was with one of his innumerable friends, is another matter. What was not in dispute was that he was about to retire with the Good Conduct medal and a pension of three shillings a day. All of his life he had been something of a 'chancer', including the time when he had forged a cheque in the name of Lord Wolseley, the Commander of the Forces in Ireland at that time; a little escapade for which he had to serve twelve months' imprisonment with hard labour. This seems to have been conveniently forgotten by the army when they gave him a Good Conduct medal on his retirement, possibly because, apart from that lapse, his army record was a clean one.

At twenty-four he had married and had taken his wife with him when he had moved to Halifax, Nova Scotia, with his regiment. She had died suddenly while they were there. Knowing what we do about him now, her death has to be regarded with deep suspicion, though the cause of her demise was never questioned by anyone.

Acting on the excuse that he was anxious to get over the deep depression that had settled over him since his wife's death, he went to England on leave, where he met and married a good-looking young woman with means of her own. He took her back to Nova Scotia where she, too, died within a short space of time. According to Dougal her death had been caused by eating poisonous oysters. With what might seem undue haste to some, Dougal had her buried within twenty-four hours so that he could get on with his life, which involved getting tied up as soon as was decently possible with a young lady who had been on good terms with his two previous wives. Once in England again, he did not bother with all the tedious paper-work involved in getting married. Instead, he used his expertise with the pen to forge a marriage certificate. Why his new 'wife' took part in the deception is anyone's guess.

In the event their association did not last for long. She decided she could not put up with his brutish behaviour any more and decided to return to Canada, from where she had originally come.

'There's only one thing,' she said. 'What shall I tell my friends?'

'Buy yourself a set of widow's weeds,' Dougal said indifferently. 'Tell them your husband died.'

She was lucky. If she had been unwise enough to stay on, she could well have ended up in an early grave like her predecessors.

Scarcely had she left than Dougal had another girl installed in his house, only for her to flee from him in the middle of the night, another victim of his violence, which he seemed to reserve for anyone who chose to fancy him at the outset.

When he left the army he eventually settled in Hassocks, where he was soon in trouble with the law and had to appear at the County Petty Sessions on an affiliation charge brought by a domestic servant who had been in his employ. The magistrates, after hearing the evidence against him, ordered Dougal to pay five shillings a week towards the support of the child. This may not sound much, but it put Dougal in an awkward position, especially as he had now lost his army pension because he had again been imprisoned for forgery in 1896. For years he had been forging people's signatures and getting away with it, as well as fathering various illegitimate children, and now at last he was beginning to suffer the consequences of his crimes.

In 1898 he met Miss Camille Holland, who must have seemed to him the ideal solution to his problems. She was fifty-six but looked nowhere near her true age, had a neat figure and exquisitely small feet of which she was particularly proud, and most important – from Dougal's point of view – she had money of her own which he hoped would shortly find its way into his pocket. An aunt had left her £7,000 which brought in from £300 to £400 in interest, and among her transactions was £400 per annum which she had invested in the publishing house of George Newnes Ltd. Living alone as she did, it was understandable that she should become the easy prey of a man like Dougal who could turn on the charm when he wanted.

They met in London while they were both staying at a boarding house in Elgin Crescent, Bayswater, and she was instantly bowled over by him. One can imagine why. When he first met Camille Holland he was still only fifty-six and looked not unlike George V, with a curling moustache that was now touched with grey, and a beard that gave him an authoritative air. He had, moreover, a captaincy, or so he said, which lent weight to anything that he had to utter.

Miss Holland was not a fool, but she was no match for Dougal who had learned that she had a substantial income of her own which he was determined should find its way into his own pockets, as it had done with his first two wives, whom he had undoubtedly poisoned, though nothing was ever proven against him.

Dougal must have been successful in his attempts to capture Miss Holland's heart, for by the following year of 1899, when they had been living together for a while, Miss Holland suddenly announced that she would like to buy a farm.

'Of course, my dear,' Dougal said. 'Nothing would please me more. We must look for a suitable habitation as soon as possible.'

They began looking around and eventually settled on an old Elizabethan farm at Clavering, which Dougal was to re-name Moat Farm. For once, Miss Holland's good business sense seems to have deserted her, as all sorts of odd stories about the place were current in the village. One of them concerned a grinning skull which actually went with the house. It was a dark and brooding house which had been owned by a lady who was doubtless delighted to get it off her hands.

As far as Miss Holland was concerned, the one disadvantage about the farm was that it was remote and lonely, the nearest village being Saffron Walden. Against this disadvantage the price of the property was only £1,550, and Dougal, who had charge of all the negotiations, saw to it that the conveyance should be in his name, although Miss Holland had to sell off some of her stock to find the money for the purchase.

The one stumbling block to the arrangements that Dougal had made was that Miss Holland announced to Dougal that there was an aspect of the legalities with which she was extremely dissatisfied. 'This won't do,' she said severely as she read through the conveyance. 'The property is conveyed to you. This must be changed so that the property is conveyed to me.'

'Leave well alone, I beg you,' Dougal pleaded. 'How can you have the conveyance in your maiden name? If it was, everyone would know that we are not married.'

'I don't care,' said Miss Holland, who was no fool when it came to matters like this. 'The conveyance must be in my name.'

Nothing would change her mind, so Dougal was forced to tear up the document and a new one was prepared, in which the farm was conveyed to her. It might have been sound business sense, but it was to cost her dear.

Before the farmhouse was ready for the new owners, they had to seek out temporary accommodation and stayed with a Mrs Wiskden in Saffron Walden, where they remained until April.

Once they had settled in, Dougal soon became totally involved in the running of the farm. He arranged for various structural alterations to be carried out and for the stagnant waters of the moat that ran around part of the farm to be filled in, and generally behaved like a man who

225

was thoroughly enjoying his new role as a gentleman farmer, as no doubt he was. To complete the picture he bought himself a horse and trap, and could often be seen driving around the neighbourhood, gracefully acknowledging whatever greetings were offered him as he passed by.

As for Camille, she bought a grand piano in London and had it sent down to the farm, where she played for her partner in the evenings when she was not busy planning what alterations she would make to the furnishings. She felt very happy with how her life had developed, and the unpleasant business about the conveyance had now been completely forgotten. However, it had not been forgotten by Dougal, who had pushed the incident to the back of his mind.

Now, with the novelty of running the farm coming to an end, Dougal had time to brood over the past, and he found that he still bitterly resented the way that Camille Holland had bested him over the matter of the property ownership. He also had the additional problem that Camille no longer held the same attraction for him that she had once had. He was one of those men whom no one woman could satisfy, and it was therefore inevitable that he would look elsewhere for a bed companion.

He found her, or so he thought in the beginning, in Florence Havies, who had joined the family as a servant only three weeks after they had taken up residence at the farm. He had put his arm around her waist and had tried to kiss her in those early days, only to have his behaviour reported to the mistress of the house, who had taken a dim view of the occurrence.

Dougal had tried to dismiss the matter with a laugh.

'She's only a kid,' he had said. 'You surely don't think I was serious?'

He later tried to force an entry into the servant girl's bedroom one night, but Miss Havies let out a piercing scream which sent him scurrying away before his lover came from her bedroom to see what was happening.

The next morning, a tight-lipped Camille met him at the breakfast table and told him she had no intention of tolerating such behaviour, and ordered him out of the house. Later that morning Camille Holland informed the servant girl that she would be going to London for a few days and would be back soon. She drove away in the trap with Dougal and was never seen again.

That same day Florence Havies wrote to her mother, asking her to come and collect her at the farm as she had become very unhappy in her present employment. When she retired to her room that night she was careful to keep her door locked, but Dougal was too busy then to bother with her.

Florence's mother arrived the following day to take her away from the farm. After a stormy scene between her and Dougal, in which he protested that his actions had been misunderstood, Florence and her mother left.

Their departure was the signal for Dougal to start bringing in a bevy of young ladies on the pretext of wanting to hire new staff. In the end the situation at the farm became the talk of the whole village. Whenever there was any inquiry about his 'wife', who had so strangely disappeared, Dougal had a whole string of answers to explain away her absence which were obviously convincing enough to keep the police from making any official inquiries.

Over the next four years the rumours about his so-called wife's disappearance continued to mount until the police could no longer ignore them, and in March 1903 Dougal finally had a visit from Superintendent Edwin Pryke. He found Dougal in a relaxed mood, because he had been lulled into a false sense of security by the passage of the years.

'Can you give me any information with a view to tracing the missing Miss Holland?' Pryke asked him.

'I have no information about her,' Dougal said easily. 'I have not seen or heard of her since I took her to Stanstead railway station more than three years ago. If you learn anything as to her whereabouts I should be pleased to hear of it. We had a tiff on the day she left, and it is unfortunate that we should have parted on those terms.'

'It is alleged that Miss Holland is shut up in a room in the house,' said Pryke. He cleared his throat. 'Do you mind me having a look round?'

'Certainly not,' Dougal said, looking the soul of co-operation. 'Go wherever you wish.'

He showed the Superintendent around the house himself, carefully pointing out anything that might be of interest to him. He was urbane and courteous and exuded a quiet self-confidence throughout his guided tour. As well he might, for he had indeed murdered Camille Holland and had buried her body so well that he was quite convinced that no one would ever find her. After all, she had been buried for the best part of four years now without being discovered and there was no reason why the situation should ever change.

All the same, the visit from the Superintendent had shaken him enough to make him decide that he should

228

make his escape from the farm as soon as possible. With that in mind he drew out all his money from two local banks, amounting to some £600. He then packed his bags and left the farm for London, where he checked in at the Central Hotel, Long Lane.

He then made the mistake of visiting the Bank of England in an attempt to exchange banknotes for gold. In this he was successful, but when he forged a cheque and the signature gave rise to suspicion, the police arrested him. Over the years he had been forging cheques and obtaining money from Camille Holland's brokers to the tune of £6,000.

When the police closed in on Dougal on 19 March 1903, he was found to be in possession of a large quantity of jewellery, most of which had belonged to Miss Holland.

The police were quite convinced that he had murdered Camille Holland. But proving it was quite a different matter.

First, they had the mammoth task of sorting out how Dougal had managed to convert all her securities into cash. He had gone about this task with extraordinary care, first selling the shares by a series of letters purporting to be from her, the proceeds of the sales being paid into Miss Holland's account, only to be later withdrawn by another series of letters authorising the withdrawal of the money in the form of cheques made out to him, or in cash.

Dougal was then taken to Moat Farm in handcuffs while the police went through the house probing every possible hiding place and ripping up floorboards, without finding anything. They even decided to drain the moat, but all that revealed was the muck of centuries that had been thrown there at some time or other and now lay buried in the mud carpeting the bottom.

It was a local journalist who knew something of the work that was carried out at the farmhouse by Dougal, who supplied the answer to what had happened to Miss Holland.

'Why don't you open up the trenches that Dougal had filled in?' he suggested to Detective Inspector Marsden who had been put in charge of the case.

'I was thinking the same thing,' Marsden agreed. 'Let's get it done as soon as possible.'

During this period Dougal had been taken each day to the courthouse at Saffron Walden where he listened continually to the requests of the police for him to be remanded each time, and when they were granted, he was then bundled into a cell to await his return to London that evening. Throughout it all, Dougal had maintained an attitude of amused contempt over the activities of the police which had got them precisely nowhere so far. It was not until they began work on one of the trenches that he suddenly became subdued.

A day or so after they had started removing the pile of rubble blocking the trench that they unearthed a woman's shoe, which was soon followed by the discovery of the clothed body of a woman, which proved to be that of Miss Holland, even though her face was now totally unrecognisable. Her dress was later identified as having been one made for Camille Holland by Mrs Wiskden, who was a seamstress by profession.

To add to the accumulation of evidence, the shoe was also identified as having been made for her by the then well-known company of Mold, shoemakers in the Edgware Road, who had a record of having made a number of shoes for Miss Holland, and which were of the same size and fitting.

How then was the murder committed? The most likely explanation is that on the day Dougal was seen driving Camille Holland to the station, after she had made her peace with him, he had, purely as a matter of expediency more than anything else, calmly shot her in the back of the head. He had then driven back to the farm and had buried her body in the ditch. It had been an easy task for him to lift the corpse from the trap and drop it into the ditch and cover it sufficiently to hide it until he had time to bury the body properly.

Dougal came up for trial at the Shire Hall in Chelmsford on Monday 22 June 1903, before Mr Justice Wright. Although the police seem to have been remarkably slow in following up Miss Holland's disappearance, they made up for it by marshalling their evidence so well that the prosecution was able to present the case against Dougal so that no one had any doubts as to his guilt. It took two days for the trial to run its course, and at the end of it he was found guilty and sentenced to death.

Dougal was duly executed on the sunny morning of 8 July 1903. Efforts to make him confess to his crime were made by the prison chaplain, who walked with him to the gallows, urging him to confess. Dougal did so at the very last moment just before the executioner pulled the lever.

The chaplain was taken to task for this display of excessive zeal. It was also brought up in the House of Commons and some form of inquiry was set afoot. The chaplain apologised and said that he was carried away by his concern for the prisoner, who was about to go to his Maker, still not in a state of grace. And there the matter was allowed to rest.

WHEN HATRED
TURNS INTO MURDER

Like so many wartime unions, Harry Dobkin's marriage to Rachel Dubinski had proved a terrible disaster from day one. After a series of spectacular rows, they eventually agreed to separate, with Rachel now spending most of her time in a small flat she had acquired for herself in Dalston, or with her sister Polly, who lived in Shoreditch. The situation had now become so bad between Dobkin and his wife that a divorce seemed the only possible solution for them.

But they had let the matter drift on for years, and now there were other problems that made a divorce out of the question. Dobkin had lost his job as a ship's steward, and since then he had turned into something of a layabout, which did nothing to improve his relationship with his wife on the rare occasions that they met. To make matters worse for them, their brief marriage had resulted in a son being born and Dobkin was forced to pay the sum of one pound a week towards the upkeep of the child. It was a small enough amount, but Dobkin bitterly resented having to pay it, so much so that he had already been to prison twice for refusing to pay up.

By the time the Second World War began he had at last managed to get a job as an auxiliary fireman. One would have thought that being in uniform might have given him a certain amount of pride in belonging to the fire service, and that he would forget his almost pathological hatred of his wife. But all he could think of was how his job might help him get rid of her.

In the event it proved to be remarkably easy, especially as Mrs Dobkin had insisted they should meet in Dalston for tea, when they would discuss her 'rights' as she called them.

According to Dobkin, when he was later interviewed by the police, the meeting was a surprisingly amicable one, especially when she had learned that he had now got a job and would be paying the maintenance money regularly. Dobkin had kept his word, and had paid the child maintenance promptly for several months, but then suddenly, without warning, collection of the payments stopped.

The clerk of the court had even made a joke about it and advised Dobkin to hang on to his money. 'I reckon you must have done your wife in,' he laughed.

When her sister informed the police that Rachel had disappeared they had not seemed unduly concerned as to what had happened to her, though they did interview Dobkin briefly on the matter. They were clearly satisfied by what he had to tell them about his last meeting with his wife so they let him go, and nothing more was heard from them until a year later when they had occasion to investigate a minor fire in a bombed-out Baptist chapel in Kennington Lane. At that time only a superficial search of the bomb site was made and nothing untoward was found.

In July 1942, a workman helping to demolish the building unexpectedly found the remains of a skeleton under the floor of the chapel cellar. Detective Inspectors Hatton and Keeling, who were called in when the discovery was made, decided at once that they were looking at a case of murder as the head of the corpse had been taken off and the limbs crudely dismembered so that the body could be accommodated beneath the flagstone covering it. Dr Keith Simpson, the well-known Home Office pathologist, was called in, and after a careful examination of the body, found that the right side of the voice box had been fractured, which led him to believe that the woman's death had been caused by strangulation.

The next obvious step was to check the Register of Missing Persons, where it was found that Rachel Dobkin, who was living apart from her husband, had been reported missing and therefore seemed the most likely person for whom they were looking.

Inspector Rawlings, who was put in charge of the case, wasted no time in getting his hands on Dobkin. 'Bring in Harry Dobkin,' he ordered. 'With a bit of luck it shouldn't be too long before we bring this case to an end.'

When Dobkin was brought in, he seemed to be highly confident. 'Don't tell me my wife has turned up after all this time,' he said, smiling.

'Your wife has been found dead in the chapel cellar of the Baptist church in Vauxhall,' Rawlings told him.

'I know nothing about that,' Dobkin said.

'That may well be true, sir. But I'm afraid I must hold you while I pursue my inquiries,' he added.

Dobkin thought for a moment, then he said quietly: 'If you've got some paper handy, I'll make a brief statement.'

Outwardly, the statement was harmless and told the police nothing. He had written the following: 'In respect of what you say that my wife has been found dead or murdered and that you say I know something I am holding back . . .'

At this point he had stopped and looked up at the expressionless face of Inspector Rawlings, not realising he had done something even more foolish than lying. He had introduced into his statement a word that had not even been used during the interview. The word was 'murdered'. There was still nothing incriminating in the statement, but the incautious use of the word 'murdered' made Rawlings more convinced than ever that they had the right man.

The rest of Dobkin's statement did nothing for his case, being no more than a rambling account of his relationship with his wife, which did not prove anything either way. He did, however, make one fatal mistake which was to cost him dear. That was when he denied ever having visited the site of the Baptist Chapel, or for that matter, that he had even heard of it. As it happened, a policeman had already reported having seen him on that particular site, and Rawlings immediately sent for him.

'Do you know this man?' he asked, indicating Dobkin.

'Of course,' the constable said. 'I know him well from the time he was fire watching at the Baptist Chapel in Kennington Lane, when I had to tell him off on several occasions for showing a light during the blackout.'

'It's a lie,' Dobkin said frantically. 'I've never seen him before in my life.'

The constable continued to insist that he had seen Dobkin on the bomb site, while Dobkin continued to deny that they had ever met before. In the end, Rawlings had no option but to send the constable on his way while attempting to quieten the now almost hysterical Dobkin, and bring the interview to an end.

To make a satisfactory case against Dobkin, Rawlings knew he would need something more substantial than a policeman's word to make it stick. He already had an X-ray photograph of the dead woman's head. He now approached Polly Dubinski who knew the name and address of her sister's dentist, and who had made a plate for her.

'Mr Barnett Kopkin has done all her dental work for years,' she told them.

They traced Mr Kopkin without any difficulty, and according to his records, he had indeed made a dental plate for Rachel. He was then taken to Guy's Hospital, where the body was lying, and was able to confirm that the dead woman was indeed Rachel Dobkin.

Further inquiries also elicited the fact that a Dr Marie Watson of the Mildmay Mission Hospital, Bethnal Green, had examined Rachel Dobkin in the October of 1939, when it was discovered that she had a fibroid growth in the uterus. As the remains found in the chapel also showed evidence that the dead woman had been suffering from the same condition, this was further proof that the body the police were holding in Guy's Hospital was that of Rachel Dobkin. Rawlings now considered that he had more than enough evidence to take Dobkin to court on the charge of murdering his wife.

On 17 November 1942, Dobkin stepped into the dock of

the Old Bailey. From the beginning it became quite obvious that he had little or no chance of walking out of the court a free man, especially after forensic pathologist Dr Keith Simpson had displayed no fewer than twenty-four points to prove that the dead woman was Rachel Dobkin. 'It is not circumstantial evidence,' Simpson said confidently. 'It is scientific evidence.'

A bald-headed man with a splayed-out nose and an unfortunate cocksure manner, Dobkin engendered a certain amount of hostility from the jurors almost from the start. However, most of his self-confident manner evaporated as he listened to Keith Simpson describe how he had come to his conclusion that the dead woman was undeniably Rachel Dobkin.

'Were you fond of your wife?' he was then asked.

'No,' said Dobkin, with a rare display of honesty.

'When did you cease to care for her?' he was then asked.

'On the day we got married,' Dobkin said. Even when his very life was in danger he could not conceal his hatred for his wife. Mr F. H. Lawton KC, acting for the defence, did his best with unpromising material to build up a defence for his client. He chose to question part of the statement made by Keith Simpson, a dangerous thing to do, especially as Simpson was an old hand at dealing with defence counsel asking him tricky questions.

'I don't disagree that the horn of a thyroid may be broken during the course of a manual strangulation,' Lawton said carefully. 'But is it not possible that a fall might break the corner of the thyroid?'

'In fifteen years I have personally examined over eleven thousand cases, and I have never seen this injury except in

238

the case of manual strangulation,' Simpson said calmly.

It was at this point that Dobkin got to his feet and asked if he could make a statement to the court, which Justice Wrottesley allowed. It turned out to be mostly a diatribe against the police who, he alleged, had done their best to rig a case against him. 'They told me under threats that if I didn't admit I killed my wife they would hang me,' he maintained.

Neither the judge nor the jury looked impressed by his statement.

'And you ask the jury to believe that, do you?' asked the judge.

'I certainly do,' Dobkin said sourly.

When did Dobkin actually kill his wife? We know from the evidence of Polly Dubinski that the last time she saw her sister was on 11 April and that her sister was going to meet Dobkin later that day. It is reasonable to suppose that he did indeed meet her, and that they had quarrelled about the money, as they had done so many times before, only this time he had lost his temper so much that he had strangled her. He had then attempted to destroy the body by means of fire with a straw mattress that was to hand, and then hacked off her head in order to bury the body under the floor of the chapel cellar, where it had remained for almost a year before being found by the workmen who had gone there to demolish the building.

All this came out in court and made his chance of escaping the hangman's noose impossible. It was therefore hardly surprising that the jurors took only twenty minutes to reach their verdict of guilty. The judge declared that he thought the jury had reached the right conclusion before placing on his wig the customary black silk and sentencing him to death.

Harry Dobkin went to his death in Wandsworth Prison on the cold morning of 27 January 1943. He went to his death without any fuss.

Dr Keith Simpson, the man whose evidence had contributed so much to Dobkin's death sentence, was given the task of carrying out the post-mortem on the body.

A FEMALE
SERIAL KILLER

Jane Toppan was born Nora Kelley in Massachusetts in 1854. She had two sisters and was one of those unfortunate people who never had a chance in life right from the start. Until her life was turned upside down by the sudden death of her mother, she was just like any well-bred girl in Boston. Her father then took on the task of bringing up the three girls. Never a strong man to begin with, he quickly collapsed under the strain and his mind gave way completely. When he was discovered one day trying to sew his eyes up he was quickly bundled away to the lunatic asylum, where he was to spend the rest of his life. The children went to their grandmother, who soon found the task of bringing them up too much for her, and the girls were taken from her care and placed in an orphanage.

In 1859 Nora was adopted by a Mr and Mrs Toppan, who gave her their name and changed her Christian name from Nora to Jane. So far, despite the stormy beginning to Jane's life there was no sign of the hereditary madness that was to take over later. Instead, she grew up to be an attractive and intelligent young lady.

Unfortunately, Jane's life was to be changed abruptly.

She got engaged to a young man who jilted her in favour of someone else. The rejection upset her badly, so much so that she attempted to commit suicide on two occasions. When these attempts failed she went into virtual seclusion for several years, before emerging from her hermit-like existence. It was at this point that Jane decided to attend a Cambridge teaching hospital not far from her home and she soon became a well-liked trainee nurse.

She was now twenty-six years old and seemingly all set to live out a normal life. To begin with all went well enough, that is until one of her patients suddenly died, although he had had nothing seriously wrong with him. When another patient in her care died shortly afterwards, Jane was called to the Chief Surgeon's office for questioning. No official complaint was made against her, but it was significant that soon afterwards she was discharged from the hospital staff.

Jane's foster parents wanted to know exactly why she had been relieved of her post. Jane did her best to reassure them. 'You have no need to worry,' she said. 'I see my task in life as looking after the old and sick, and comforting them in their neediest hour.'

From 1880 until 1901 Jane went from job to job, and during that period a series of patients died while in her care, but we have no record of any complaints being made about her. She had learnt her lesson in the Cambridge hospital, and as a result she had become much more careful. Apart from that, all her patients were now private ones, cared for in their own homes, where she was able to nurse them without medical supervision. It was also an age when it was easier for nurses to get away with murder than it is now.

In 1901 nurses were even less carefully scrutinised than

today. Qualifications were minimal and it was not long before Jane found herself nursing a patient named Mattie Davis who died suddenly while in her care. Three other members of her family died soon afterwards. Even then no one seems to have suspected anything, and spoke only of Jane's touching devotion to the family, and how she had been quite happy to sit by their bedsides until the end. Furthermore, she had volunteered to stay on for a while to look after the remaining members of the family.

When Captain Gibbs, a family relative, who had just returned from a sea voyage, suddenly arrived on the scene, matters were to change dramatically. When he learned the shattering news that his wife was among those who had died, he called in the police to investigate their mysterious deaths. Unlike the others, he did not share their enthusiasm for Jane Toppan. He had suggested to her that there should be a series of post-mortems, but Jane did not take kindly to this idea.

'Such practices are against the religious beliefs of the family,' she told the Captain.

By this time Jane Toppan had wiped out the whole family, and there was no one left to support her argument and the autopsies were therefore duly performed, when it was discovered that they had all been killed by morphine poisoning. Jane had always maintained that all their deaths had been brought about by a stroke. However, by the time the police and the authorities had carried out all their inquiries and went looking for her, she had already fled.

Although she was away from her old haunts, Jane Toppan had kept her hand in by finishing off her foster sister, Mrs Edna Bannister, before moving on yet again to

243

nurse the Nichols family who lived in New Hampshire.

In her absence, the police had been examining the bodies of dozens of the people who had died while under her tender care. In every case the police found that all her patients had died from either morphine or atropine poisoning. They also discovered that she had acquired a vast amount of poison by using forged prescriptions which purported to have been signed by imaginary doctors. Clearly, Jane was expecting a long and successful career as a mass poisoner.

Jane Toppan, meanwhile, was still proceeding along her merry way, poisoning her patients whenever she could, until the day inevitably came when she opened the door of the Nichols' family home to find Detective Whitney standing outside.

'Are you Nurse Jane Toppan?' he asked.

'I am,' she said warily. 'What do you want?'

'I want you,' the detective said calmly. 'You are wanted for questioning in connection with a series of murders that took place in Massachusetts.'

Taxed with the murders, Jane openly confessed to killing all her patients. 'I fooled them all,' she said proudly. 'I fooled those stupid doctors, and I fooled their stupid relatives. I have been fooling them all for years and years.'

Nurse Toppan's confession was notable for its complete indifference to the people she had killed, though she did say afterwards that the killings had been carried out in such a way as to make her victims just fall asleep and never wake up. 'I have been accused of using arsenic,' she declared. 'That is quite ridiculous. If I had used arsenic, they would have died hard deaths. After all, I couldn't bear to see them suffer, and often it took days for them to die.'

On 25 July 1902 Jane Toppan was put on trial for her life, though it was obvious from the murders she had committed that she was hopelessly insane; a fact that was supported in a statement from Dr Stedman, the psychiatrist who had examined her in prison. 'In my opinion Jane Toppan is suffering from a form of insanity that cannot be cured,' he announced.

Instead of gratefully accepting his statement as a lifeline, Jane's reaction was one of high indignation. 'The alienist lies,' she shouted to the court. 'I am not crazy, and you know it. I know right from wrong. That proves I am sane,' she concluded triumphantly.

Fortunately for her, the jury disagreed with her, and she was sent to the Taunton State Asylum for the Criminally Insane for the rest of her life.

In the interim period she was again interviewed in jail by the psychiatrist, Dr Stedman, to whom she was quite happy to admit that she had killed more than thirty of her patients. The general opinion at the time was that she had been far too modest in her estimate, the total being more likely to have been a hundred.

In the asylum her mood and behaviour ranged from the morose and suicidal (when she would accuse the nurses of trying to poison her) to long periods when she was tractable and amenable to suggestion.

The years rolled by until outwardly she became a sweet, white-haired old lady who looked as if she wouldn't hurt a fly. She lived until 17 August 1938, when she died at the age of eighty-four. It says much for the devotion of the nurses who came and went over the years and managed to look after her so well that she survived that long.

It is amazing how many there were like her in those days when Jane Toppan was busy finishing off her patients. What is surprising is how progressive the law was in its attitude to the nurses who became murderers. The law in those days may not have known much about the mental condition that made people like Jane Toppan behave in the way they did, but at least it recognised that it would only be an act of gratuitous cruelty to inflict punishment on a person who was mentally deranged.

THE
KILLER POLICEMAN

When Catherine McCluskey's body was found lying dead
in a Glasgow street in the early hours of 28 July 1950,
the first assumption of the taxi driver who had found
her was that she was the victim of a hit and run driver,
a view that was at first shared by the police officer who
had been summoned to the spot. However, the officer
soon revised his opinion. In road accidents of this nature
you would expect to find broken glass lying around the
site where the incident was supposed to have occurred;
here there was none. And, although her jaw had been
fractured, along with numerous other injuries to her
body and face, there were no leg injuries. Professor
Andrew Allison of St Mungo's College, Glasgow, confirmed that it was more likely that Catherine had not
been knocked down, but had been killed and then dumped
in Prospecthill Road, where the body had been found.
What had seemed to be nothing more than a routine
hit and run accident had now turned into a case of
murder.

First, the police looked into the life and circumstances
of the victim. It transpired that she was a forty-year-old

unmarried mother who lived in a slum tenement in south Glasgow. It was found that she had had many acquaintances, and included among them was a Glasgow policeman named James Ronald Robertson, who had been a close friend for many years.

Once they found out about Robertson, it was only a matter of time before they arrested him for the murder of Catherine McCluskey, with whom they knew Robertson had been having an affair.

Robertson was that very rare animal – a rogue policeman who had been in the force for five years, and was known to his colleagues as being very much a ladies' man, whose sexual activities among the local girls had often been covered up by his fellow officers, who looked on his busy sex life with some amusement until they remembered that Robertson had been having an affair with Catherine McCluskey.

Their amusement quickly turned to horror once they found out that Robertson had suddenly become the most likely suspect in a murder case. Friends who had helped him in the past now wanted nothing to do with him and, in fact, actively avoided him whenever possible. From being a reasonably well-liked officer, he had become someone who was now looked upon with the gravest suspicion. Those who knew him well remembered the stories they had heard of how he had become the father of a baby boy and was paying out eight shillings a week towards the child's upkeep.

It was at this point that Inspector McDougall began an investigation into Robertson's life. Outwardly, he had led a life of blameless respectability as a family man with two children, a boy and a girl. But women were the cause of Robertson's downfall.

On 25 July, two nights before the murder was committed, he had been on duty with a constable named Douglas Moffat, who remembered that on that night Robertson had said he was meeting someone whom he described as a blonde, attractive woman. He then went off to keep his assignation and returned in due course saying that the meeting had gone off well enough.

On the night of the murder, Robertson was again on duty with Moffat, to whom he had announced that he was going off to see his blonde lady friend, but that he would not be away for so long this time.

'I didn't see Robertson for nearly two hours,' Moffat said to the Inspector who was questioning him. 'When he did appear I couldn't help noticing that his collar was soaked with sweat and that he seemed very agitated.' Moffat also noticed that Robertson's trousers were dusty, and that the toe-caps of his boots were scraped.

Listening to all this it became obvious that Robertson was their man. Inspector McDougall and a number of other police officers left the station to seek him out. They found him performing his duties on the beat in the normal way and promptly arrested him, while a party of detectives went on to his house where they found a number of car registration books and some car keys. All of them had been stolen and proved that Robertson was indulging in a series of petty crimes when the opportunity presented itself.

Robertson had been using a black Austin car to get himself to and from work, and this was towed away by the police to their garage for examination. Anticipating that he would be arrested as soon as it was learned the car had been stolen, Robertson readily confessed that he had found it abandoned and taken possession of it and fitted it with false number plates.

Robertson was remanded in custody in connection with the theft of the car, though of course this was only a minor offence compared to that of the murder of Catherine McCluskey, which the police were hoping to pin on him. As it happened, Robertson had no sooner admitted to stealing the Austin, than he was already admitting that Catherine McCluskey's death had been caused by the car. After he had admitted that, he then went on to pour out the whole sordid story. It was as if he now had a terrible compulsion to rid himself of his guilt by confessing to everything the police wanted to know about the events leading up to the murder.

He had first met Catherine McCluskey when he had been called to a house in Nicholson Street to quell a disturbance. From that point onwards he had remained on good terms with her, though he denied ever having gone to her flat again after their first meeting.

On the night of the murder, Robertson had admitted to having seen Catherine McCluskey. That evening she had told him that her Indian landlord had locked her out of her flat as she was now several weeks in arrears with the rent. She had then asked him to drive her to Neilston, a village several miles away where she had friends who would put her up until she had sorted out her financial affairs. Not daring to risk going so far away from his beat, Robertson had refused, at which point Catherine had burst into tears.

They were driving aimlessly around when Catherine then asked him to drive her to a house in Rutherglen Road, which was much nearer to his beat.

Again Robertson had to refuse her. 'I just can't take the chance of not being on my beat if someone from the station comes looking for me, as they so often do.' He thought about it for a few seconds, and then added, 'I'm going back to the station. If you'd like to come with me I suggest you make up your mind quickly, otherwise you'll find yourself walking home.'

According to Robertson, her mood of depression had passed, and she asked to be let out of the car. If anything, she now made light of her troubles, and she made off towards her flat in the hope that she might be allowed in to collect some clothing she had left behind.

His story so far had been convincing enough and quite believable. It was only from that point onwards that the police looked on what he had to say with the darkest suspicion. Robertson said that no sooner had he left her than he began worrying about leaving her alone and stranded. As he had only gone a matter of a few yards, rather than turn the car round, he had simply backed up the car fairly rapidly, when he felt a jar. He had stopped the car immediately and was in the act of getting out, when to his horror, he saw Catherine McCluskey lying beneath the running board.

'Her mouth was full of blood,' Robertson said with some emotion. 'Once I had satisfied myself that she was dead, I then tried to extricate her clothing, moving the car back and forth in an attempt to clear the body. Eventually, I found the body lying free at the back of the vehicle.'

251

The story had been carefully worked out, but it wasn't good enough to satisfy the police. 'What then?' he was asked.

'I was in a hopeless situation,' Robertson said. 'In the end I just started up the car and drove away.'

It was obvious from the expressions of the bevy of detectives who were questioning him, that none of them believed him. 'If the woman's death was accidental, as you say it was, all you had to do was to summon help,' one of the detectives coldly pointed out to him.

When Robertson was arrested a heavy cosh had been found on him, and everyone working on the case was agreed that he had hit the girl in a fit of temper, and that he had then driven the car backwards and forwards over her body before making off.

If this was then an act of premeditated murder, as the evidence now seemed to indicate, the reason for it did not emerge until Robertson went on trial when he admitted that he had killed Catherine McCluskey because he was frightened that his relationship with her had become common knowledge and would ruin his career. This may sound little enough motive for committing murder, but then we do not know the whole story to this very day. Had the woman decided that she wanted Robertson to marry her, and perhaps put pressure on him by threatening to tell the police authorities that he was the father of one of her children? We shall never know.

Robertson was brought to trial in November 1950, when he stuck very much to the story he had already told. Robertson's uniform was the main piece of evidence presented by the prosecution. Robertson had already told the court how he had tried to free Catherine McCluskey's body from beneath the car. How could he have done this, the prosecution asked pointedly, without getting a single spot of blood anywhere on his uniform?

Robertson's cosh was also examined by Professor Allison, who found a small stain on it. He had at first thought that the stain was human blood but could not prove it with any degree of certainty. The ever-obliging Robertson volunteered the information that the blood on it had been acquired when he had been called out to deal with a fracas and he had occasion to use the cosh. The blood on it certainly did not belong to Catherine McCluskey, he claimed, and this eventually proved to be the case.

The Glasgow medico-forensic expert, Professor John Glaister, was also called in to give evidence and to reconstruct how the woman had died. 'The body must have been relaxed and in a recumbent position,' he said. 'As for the injuries to her knees, these are nothing more than gravel rash or abrasions.'

Mr Cameron KC, acting for the defence, had examined the Austin car that Robertson had been driving, and had noticed a small dent in the boot which had suggested to him the possibility that Robertson had indeed run down McCluskey accidentally while driving backwards.

Glaister, cross-examined on this point, had to agree that it was a possibility. 'But then it would have produced a very large bruise – larger than any found on the body. Such a bruise had not been one of the woman's many injuries,' he added as a rider.

'But the dent could still have been produced by contact with the bone?' he persisted.

'I have said that I could not eliminate it,' Glaister said. 'But I would have expected skin damage overlying that part of the bone involved.'

The seven-day trial was coming to an end, but first they had to hear the evidence of Dr Walter Weir, a pathologist from the local hospital who had examined both the knees and the head of the dead woman. 'The injuries she received to her head were inflicted before death,' he informed the court. 'But those to both knees were made after death,' he added.

As two other pathologists were then produced by the defence, who claimed the woman's injuries had been caused in the way that Robertson had described, nothing much could be proven one way or another on this point.

The defence then produced Charles Wicks, an Edinburgh consulting engineer, who supported Robertson's claim as to how the sequence of events had occurred. He did, however, also put forward a suggestion that only served to weaken Robertson's case.

'The shaft in the Austin is enclosed,' he said. 'Therefore I don't see how it was possible for her clothing to have become entangled with the engine.'

There was nothing straightforward in this case. But at the end of the trial, Robertson confessed to the court that he had been a liar and a thief, and a man who had often neglected his duty, all for the sake of the women he had pursued. When Robertson confessed to having killed McCluskey to avert the danger of being thrown out of the police force, everything began to make sense.

He was found guilty by a majority verdict, something that is permitted in Scottish law, and was sentenced to death. He was hanged on 16 December 1950.

THE HOME
OF NO RETURN

When Amelia Amy Archer opened a nursing home for the care of elderly people in Windsor, Connecticut, everyone agreed that she had made a good choice of location for that sort of establishment, as it was a genteel town, full of retired people. The town itself was pleasant enough, with dozens of tree-lined streets with gracious-looking Victorian houses occupied mostly by people whose only vice was an occasional glass of elderberry wine. The elderly citizens were cared for by a host of doctors, also retired and well past their best, who would therefore be happy to support Sister Amy, as she was known, and be prepared to sign a death certificate when needed.

Amy Archer arrived in Windsor one day in April 1907, after she had purchased a large and forbidding-looking mansion which she informed everyone she met that she was opening as The Archer Home for Elderly People and Chronic Invalids. Accompanying her was her husband, known affectionately to Amy Archer as Big Jim, and whose function in the nursing home was to fetch and carry and empty and wash out the bedpans. There were to be no servants, Sister Amy intending to do all the nursing and cooking herself.

The Archer Home was soon operating at full stretch and was occupied by five elderly gentlemen and four elderly women. In addition, there was also a much younger man who looked so ill all the time that the general conclusion was that he had to be in the last stages of consumption.

Sister Amy must have been coining money hand over fist, because she had come to what was a highly satisfactory arrangement with all her charges. In exchange for only paying her a very small stipend but making their wills over to her, she guaranteed to look after them and provide whatever medical attention was necessary for the rest of their natural lives. As the rates for her boarding charges were extraordinarily cheap, the old people's relatives were only too glad to entrust their loved ones to her care.

To make the nursing home a going concern, it was essential that her patients should not live long enough to become a drain on Sister Amy's coffers. To make sure they didn't linger around too long, she quietly poisoned or smothered them, one by one, at regular intervals, thereby keeping the staff of the local churchyard busy burying them. Death generally occurred at night so as not to make it too obvious that there seemed to be an abnormally high death rate.

Unfortunately for all concerned, Sister Amy then hit on an idea that would improve her finances even more. She would kill off her husband and then marry one of her elderly patients, who would be delighted to be marrying a still far from old woman when he had thought that such dimly remembered pleasures were now beyond his reach for ever. After a suitable lapse of time, he too, would be sent on his way with a dose of skilfully administered poison from her medicine cupboard. But first there was Big Jim in the way, who had to be got rid of quickly.

While she was waiting for the appropriate moment to send Big Jim to his grave, Sister Amy had a surprise visit from Michael Gilligan, a man with a bulbous nose brought on by too much drinking. He was in his mid-thirties, with a roguish smile and a charming voice which he used to great effect on Sister Amy, who was easily influenced by that sort of thing. She listened sympathetically to his hard luck story.

'You poor thing,' she exclaimed when he had finished. 'Do come right in and I'll fix you up with something to eat.'

After finishing off a hearty meal, Gilligan offered to look around the nursing home to see if there was anything he could do to improve it. 'I'm a handy man, I am, with tools, and there's plenty I'm sure I could do with this place. If you'd like to give me board and lodgings until I'm finished, I could fix this place up a treat.'

The upshot of it all was that Gilligan moved in and was soon busy ripping up floors and tearing down partitions. All this activity Big Jim noticed with ill grace. He could not help but see that Gilligan tippled heavily while about the premises, without incurring any displeasure from Sister Amy who had laid down that on no account should Big Jim be seen drinking. This was something Big Jim resented. In the end he could stand it no longer. 'We won't be needing you no more,' he said to Gilligan.

'No, is that a fact?' Gilligan said. 'Who says so?'

'I do,' Big Jim told him.

Gilligan's answer to that was to report the matter to

Sister Amy, who realised that Big Jim had now clearly outstayed his welcome. She laid her plans accordingly, first going to her nearest neighbours, the Bliss sisters, who seemed to spend most of their days peering through the lace curtains and watching everything they could of what was going on at Sister Amy's nursing home. Because of their close proximity, Sister Amy had taken good care to be on friendly terms with them, even to the extent of running herself ragged going over and looking after one of the sisters when she had gone down with pneumonia.

One April morning after Gilligan had been installed in Sister Amy's home for a couple of months, she called on the Bliss sisters, a social event she had been carrying out ever since the nursing home had opened. Normally she had presented a cheerful exterior, but on this occasion it was obvious that she was not her usual happy self.

'Whatever is the matter?' asked one of the sisters.

'It's my husband,' Sister Amy said tearfully. 'I'm afraid he's not long for this world.'

'How awful!' the sisters chorused.

'I'm afraid it's the drink that has done it . . .' She lowered her voice. 'The truth of the matter is that he's been a secret drinker for years. To my shame I never knew it. It's too late now, of course. He has these terrible stomach pains. There's hardly a night passes when he doesn't have one of those awful haemorrhages.'

'Have you thought of calling in the doctor?'

'It's no use,' Sister Amy said, making a show of bravely fighting back her tears. 'I'm a nurse, and I know when a person is too far gone for anything to be done.' She looked at them despairingly. 'If only Jim had given me some

warning I might still have been able to save him. As it is—'
Leaving the sentence unfinished, she gave them a brave
little smile and left soon afterwards, well aware she had put
in some valuable spade work on the Bliss sisters.

As for Big Jim, he had been unhappy for some time
about the state of affairs that existed between himself and
Sister Amy. Not a talkative man by nature, he was,
however, disposed to talk about his problems among his
friends when he went off on one of his secret drinking
sessions with them. 'I'm not a happy man,' he informed
them in his County Mayo brogue. 'It's that wife of mine,
you see. I can't satisfy that woman at nights, much as I try.
Her demands are too much for any normal man, let alone
for someone like me who believes a little is all right, but too
much of it can destroy a man.' He looked at his listeners
despairingly. 'I just don't know how long I'm going to keep
up with it all.'

A few days later, Sister Amy posted off the monthly
letters from her charges to their relatives, all of them
having been written by Sister Amy herself. Not surprisingly, all the letters were glowing paeons of praise for the
nursing home and the good food that was being served up
to them.

The death rate at the home was now becoming alarming
and upset all the available statistics on residential homes
for the elderly and infirm. Even Big Jim had by now gone
on his way, helped by a judicious extra dose of poison to
expedite matters. As for Sister Amy, she had been
inconsolable for weeks, banging out *Nearer My God to
Thee* on the organ for hours on end.

Then one day the whole situation changed when Sister

Amy burst into the Bliss house with a piece of monumental news . . . 'Congratulate me!' she cried. 'I'm the happiest woman in the world.' She paused for breath, and then all the words came out in a rush. 'Mr Gilligan has asked me to become his wife,' she announced. 'Isn't that marvellous?'

The Bliss sisters agreed it was indeed marvellous news, and wished her all the very best for the future, and Amy went off happily to plan a new life for herself. There was no intention now of marrying one of the old gentlemen in residence and then finishing him off quietly with a dose of poison.

'Brother Gilligan' as Sister Amy was fond of calling her new husband, had much more get up and go in him than Big Jim had ever had. He was a much more forcible character, and continued to drink openly in front of Sister Amy, who always tried to make excuses for him. 'He needs it for his health,' she said fondly one day to some of her friends. Gilligan, however, had a more basic reason for needing to drink. 'She's quite a woman to take care of at nights, and she knows that I'm the man for the job. The booze is to help me keep up my strength.'

Gilligan may have felt himself to be on safe ground with Sister Amy, and there is no doubt that he could have had a long run with her – that is if nature (or booze) had not suddenly played a cruel trick on him. Just at a time when he was congratulating himself on having the situation nicely under control, Gilligan found himself to be impotent. Of course, this was only to be expected in view of his intake of alcohol, and the complete reverse of his ill-informed opinion of the role of drink on his libido. It was a terrible blow to a man like Gilligan and it thoroughly upset him. His distress was still nothing to the grief that it caused Sister Amy when she learned that her husband was no longer the man he had once been. Being a realist, she wasted no time going about with a long face and bemoaning to all and sundry that her husband was no longer of much help to her in the house. Perhaps there was a brief moment of regret when she fed him a dose of poison. If this was indeed the case, she got over his sudden demise with remarkable speed. No sooner was he under the ground than she was already making overtures to a sprightly old gentleman named Runyon, who seemed the most likely contender to become her new husband. He was a lively man with a vigorous voice and a nice line in Irish songs that would surely keep the residents of the nursing home happy in the evenings, and would make a welcome change from having to go through the usual repertoire of uplifting hymns.

At about this time a new arrival came to the nursing home. His name was Andrews, and he was a vigorous-looking man who did not look anything like his age. Sister Amy was taken with him immediately, and for a while Runyon was kept strictly in the background, where he was held as very much of a reserve player so to speak – that is until she made the mistake of trying to flirt with Andrews one day.

'You're a very attractive man,' Sister Amy said, clasping him affectionately by the arm.

'Please don't do that,' Andrews said, gently disengaging himself.

'What's the matter? Don't you like me?'

'It's not that,' Andrews replied. 'If you must know, I prefer the company of men.'

'Well I never,' Sister Amy said, and she drifted away, her mind a mass of conflicting thoughts. The slight problem of how she was going to be able to murder both Runyon and Andrews without causing undue comment, occupied her mind for the rest of that day. She was by nature an impatient woman, and as the two men had become an embarrassment to her, she wanted them both out of the way as quickly as possible.

When it came to the point, Sister Amy managed things with remarkable ease, first quietly smothering Andrews and then poisoning Runyon. One way and another it had been a particularly stressful time for her, and she had needed all her strength and resolution to carry it all through.

Ever since the nursing home had opened its doors to the public some six years previously there had never been a shortage of people to fill the void whenever a patient died. In the cases of Runyon and Andrews, their places were filled almost immediately by some people called Gowdy, who seemed to have no sooner moved in than they were on their way to the graveyard, the two of them having died within three hours of one another.

The trouble was that this time Sister Amy had over-reached herself, causing even the Bliss sisters to remark that her charges seemed to die at an unnatural rate. Not that they appeared to have the slightest suspicion yet that Sister Amy was running some sort of murder factory, but the truth of the matter was that with such a long series of successful killing behind her, Sister Amy had become over-confident and therefore careless.

She was now even preparing to marry one of her

residents. The lucky man, who was named Charles Smith, couldn't believe it when she told him that she would be delighted to marry him, providing he made her his sole beneficiary. Within a few short months he, too, was dead, but not before he had made everything over to Sister Amy.

All in all, she had disposed of over forty people, not including her various husbands, and at long last people began to talk. Windsor being such a small town, it was not long before the gossip reached the ears of the police who started making some inquiries, as did a number of reporters, including one by the name of Mike Toughy, who launched full-scale inquiries into the affairs of the Archer Home for Elderly People.

What he learned seemed to confirm his suspicions that something was seriously amiss at the nursing home, where the death rate was so far above the average that it demanded an immediate investigation.

At first his research got him nowhere. First he went to see the doctors who had issued the death certificates. Not surprisingly, they had nothing to add to what was already on the certificates.

With a fine disregard for the legalities of what he was doing, Toughy then bribed a couple of gravediggers to dig up Andrews' body. The report that he got from the laboratory in Boston, where he had sent a small portion of the corpse was disappointing. They found nothing that could lead anyone to suspect that Andrews had been poisoned.

Toughy then had two more bodies dug up, but again neither of them showed any traces of poison. Clearly, Sister

Amy had taken to smothering some of her victims while they were asleep.

All this had taken up a certain amount of time without Toughy getting anywhere. Meanwhile, Sister Amy was at it again, her latest victim being a middle-aged man, but this time she changed her method, sending him on his way with a dose of rat poison. Unfortunately for her, Toughy had now hired a commercial artist, who had done a number of lightning sketches of Sister Amy as she bustled in and out of her house. These were passed around the local chemists with instructions to let him know if anyone resembling Sister Amy had been in to purchase poison.

In due course, Sister Amy went into a chemist and ordered a large supply of arsenic. Armed with this information Toughy went to see the State's Attorney, who immediately ordered more bodies to be exhumed. This time, they were all found to be riddled with arsenic.

She was arrested and put on trial at the Hartford Court House, Connecticut, on 17 June 1917, after ten years of a highly successful and lucrative career as a mass murderer. She maintained her innocence throughout, claiming that she had had the interests of her patients at heart, and that she had always followed the tenets of the Christian Church in all her dealings with her patients. To see her standing in the dock, a demure little figure, carrying a small bible in one hand, it must have been difficult to believe what she had done.

The judge, however, had no such misgivings, and sentenced her to death by hanging. This time, as is so often the case with murder trials in the States, she managed to get herself a second trial on a technical fault, and got life instead.

She was due to serve out her life sentence in Weatherfield Prison, but then she began to have fits. After she had tried to poison the warden and a number of her jailors she was packed off to a lunatic asylum, where she was kept in a padded cell for the rest of her life until she died in 1928 at the age of fifty-nine.

THE
LUTON SACK MURDER

On 19 November 1943 two men were on their way to work when they saw some sacking lying among the rubbish that had gathered at that part of the River Lea. When they brought it to the surface and opened it, they saw that it contained the trussed-up and naked body of a woman who had been strangled. Her face had been beaten to a near pulp, which seemed to suggest her murderer had committed this gratuitous piece of violence in order to make it difficult to identify her.

All that Chief Inspector Chapman was able to find out about her was that she had been somewhere in the region of thirty-five and had been pregnant at the time of her murder, and that she had been pregnant at least once before. Apart from those few facts there had been no other clues to her identity.

With no distinguishing marks on the body to help the police to identify her, they had to resort to showing gruesome pictures of her in the press, and having enlargements of the body flashed on to the screens of the local cinemas. Although one of these was seen by her teenage daughter, it was hardly surprising that she did not recognise her mother. The two sons, aged fifteen and sixteen respectively, and who had time to examine the photograph of their mother when it was shown in the front of a local shop window, decided that it could be their mother. They mentioned this fact to their father, who told them it could not have been their mother as she had called at the house while they were at school to collect some extra clothes on the way to her brother's house in Grantham.

The police went through their list of missing persons and 404 missing women were either traced or excluded from their inquiries. Chief Inspector Chapman then had pictures of the dead woman shown to hundreds of houseowners in the hope that someone might identify her. It was only after this, too, had failed to get a response that Chapman had an unexpected piece of luck. He came across a dog gnawing away at a piece of black cloth which the animal had pulled out of a rubbish heap near to where the body had been found. By an incredible piece of good fortune, it turned out to be a piece of a coat which had been dyed by a local branch of Sketchley's, and which still bore a just discernible number on it. Sketchley's books quickly revealed that the customer had been Mrs Rene Manton of Regent Street, Luton, who had had the coat dyed for a funeral some months earlier.

As he had just completed a house-to-house search without any luck, he went to the address in Regent Street, where a small girl opened the door to him. Despite the fact that he had only seen the mutilated body of the dead woman, with the face barely recognisable, the little girl was nevertheless so similar to her that he was convinced he was looking at Rene Manton's daughter.

Trying to control his mounting excitement, Chapman said as calmly as he could: 'Is your mother at home?'

'She's not here,' he was told. 'She's gone away for a while to stay with her brother at Grantham.'

Chapman then went to see Rene Manton's half-blind mother, Mrs Minnie Bavister, who fortunately lived quite nearby. Mrs Bavister was quite convinced that her daughter was still alive and well. 'My daughter has written to me several times recently,' she told him.

'May I see those letters?' Chapman asked her.

'Of course.' She went away and returned a few minutes later with the letters which she handed to Chapman. 'It's such a pity that she and Bertie never seem to have got on well,' she sighed. 'It's not the first time she has left him, you know. The last time she was gone for the best part of five months before she came back.'

'Are you sure these letters were written by your daughter?' Chapman asked her.

'Of course. As you know, I can't see too well these days, so I get someone to read them out to me. They're from her all right.'

Chapman studied the letters with great interest. One of them had only been written a week ago and carried a London postmark on the envelope.

After leaving Mrs Bavister, taking the letters with him, Chapman decided that a chat with Bertie Manton was overdue. He therefore went to the National Fire Station where he had learned that Manton worked as a driver.

By the time Chapman spoke to Manton he had already found out quite a lot about him, including the fact that he had been a professional lightweight boxer when he had been a young man, and that he was still something of a keep-fit fanatic. Chapman had also been to see Rene Manton's sister, who had given him a vivid picture of Rene's life with Bertie Manton, which by all accounts was no bed of roses. Potentially a violent man, he was always quarrelling with his wife and was known to have even physically attacked her.

There was no sign of this side of Manton's nature when he was confronted by Chapman. If anything, he presented himself to the Inspector as a fairly meek and mild character, deserving of some sympathy for being married to a woman who had not been above playing around with other men behind his back.

Chapman then decided to let Manton stew in his own juice while he went off to see Mrs Manton's dentist, whose name and address he had managed to obtain from him.

Like most dentists, he kept detailed records, including the plaster cast he had made for her plate, which was missing when the body had been discovered. The cast exactly fitted the description of the original dental plate made for her by the dentist, and it was quite enough for Chapman to go back to the Fire Station in Luton, where he arrested Bertie Manton for the murder of his wife.

The clincher, as far as Chapman was concerned, had occurred at their first meeting, when Manton had shown him letters purporting to have been written by his wife. In two of them the name Hampstead had been written without the letter 'p'. Chapman had then asked Manton to write something so that the police would have a record of his handwriting.

'What shall I write?' Manton had asked him.

'Oh, I don't know,' Chapman said. 'Try this.' He dictated a short sentence which contained the word Hampstead. When Manton spelt the word Hampstead, he again wrote it without the 'p'. Chapman knew then that he had his man, but he also knew that he would need much more than this to prove to any court of law that Manton was the murderer.

Fortunately, when taxed with the crime, Manton readily confessed to having murdered his wife. 'I'm sorry I told you all those lies about my wife,' he said. 'I killed her, but it was only because I lost my temper. I had gone home for lunch, and over a cup of tea Rene jumped up and flung her tea in my face. She shouted at me and said she hoped it would blind me. This was enough to make me completely lose my temper. I picked up a nearby heavy stool and hit her about the head and face. It was only later when I came to my senses that I realised what I had done.'

There was more about his wife and how generally bad-tempered she was and how she had become quite impossible to live with. She was, moreover, pregnant with a child she didn't want and was often openly hostile to him without cause.

'I only put up with her because of the children,' Manton confessed to him.

All this painted Bertie Manton as the victim of an unfortunate marriage which had turned sour; something that was very far from being the case. The real truth of the matter was that Manton was a man with an ungovernable temper, who had murdered his wife in a moment of insane fury. Unlike so many murderers who have killed in a moment of blind rage, Manton's subsequent behaviour was so cold and calculating as to forfeit any sympathy he might have got from the jury.

As it had been lunchtime and the children were at school, he was able to work methodically, stripping the body of everything that might lead to her identification, even down to her rings. Then he mutilated her face still further, stowed the body in some sacking and dragged it down to the cellar to be disposed of later. The rest of that afternoon was spent in cleaning up the blood that was everywhere.

In the early evening he packed the children off to the cinema, with the exception of his daughter Ivy, who went off to tea with one of her friends.

No detail seemed to have been missed by him. He destroyed his wife's dental plate which he had found in a glass of water feeling, rightly enough, that someone might think it strange that she had gone off without it. The stool which he had used to kill his wife had been broken when he had repeatedly struck her. He looked at it thoughtfully and then when his son Richard came home he handed it to him. 'We're short of wood,' he told him. 'Break it up for firewood and use it to light the fire.'

What followed then was something that might have been taken from some macabre thriller. After trussing up the body and taking it to the cellar, cleaning the house and making sure the children were out of the way, he carried the body upstairs and placed it over the handlebars of his bicycle. With it perched precariously thus he then calmly trundled through the town and down to the river, where he dumped the corpse in the shallow water.

This must have needed considerable strength, but being extremely fit and strong, Manton had managed it without misadventure. One can imagine, though, what his feelings must have been throughout his journey, when it only needed a chance encounter with a friend, or the bad luck of being stopped by a policeman, anxious to know what was in the sack, for his plan to rid himself of the corpse to have gone completely awry. He had made no mistakes, and it was only thanks to the dogged determination of Inspector Chapman that he was ever caught at all.

He was tried at the Bedford Assizes, where he appeared before Mr Justice Singleton, a judge of the old school who was clearly not impressed by Bertie Manton.

To start with, Manton had begun his defence by portraying himself as an inoffensive man who had been driven to committing murder because of his wife's constant infidelities with the local soldiery who had infested the area since the beginning of the war.

Justice Singleton listened with ill-concealed impatience to Manton's attempts to blacken his wife's name. 'Bear in mind when you are filled with pity for the man on trial, that not much has been said for the one who is dead,' he warned the jury. 'We have only his account of why they parted,' he went on. 'What would the woman have said if she had been alive? You may wonder whether she was as black as he has said.'

The noted pathologist Keith Simpson did much to destroy Manton's picture of himself as a non-violent man who had become the unfortunate victim of circumstance. 'I found strangulation marks on Mrs Manton's throat, which would seem to prove that an attempt was made to strangle her while she was still alive,' he declared. 'It is my opinion that she had been pinned against the wall with Manton's hands around her throat. She managed to escape, only to be caught again. This time she was battered to death with a heavy stool. If my conclusions are correct, Manton's story of picking up the stool and hitting her with it in a fury does not stand up.'

Keith Simpson's picture of what he thought had happened did a great deal of harm to Manton, who was no longer seen as a non-violent man, but instead someone who had gone to a great deal of trouble to cover his tracks, when any man committing a murder as a result of a fit of temper would have gone for help.

When it became clear to the jury they found him guilty and the judge sentenced him to death. As was so often the case when the death penalty had been passed, there was the usual outcry against execution being carried out. In the case of Bertie Manton there were 300,000 signatures on a petition for mercy submitted to the Home Office, and this time the petition was accepted. Manton was reprieved and sent to Parkhurst Prison on the Isle of Wight to serve out a life sentence. He died in 1947, after having served approximately three years of his sentence.

DEATH
ON THE HIGH SEAS

James Camb was a good-looking man with an oversized sexual urge that made any young woman who came his way a potential victim of his often uncontrollable passions. As the deck steward on the ocean-going liner *Durban Castle*, he had ample opportunity to have more than his fair share of conquests among the passengers, many of whom were not above having an affair with one of the crew. This long string of flirtations, generally carried to their successful conclusion, had made him cocky and self-assured, so that when an obscure young actress came aboard the ship at Cape Town, Camb, who was always on the look-out for a new encounter, saw her as soon as she came aboard and immediately marked her out as his next potential conquest.

Gay, or to give her her official name, Eileen Isabella Ronnie Gibson was not a happy young woman when she boarded the *Durban Castle*. Recently she had begun to suffer from fainting fits and had decided to leave the company of *Golden Boy*, a play written by Clifford Odets in which she had played opposite the boxer Eric Boon. She had suspected she was pregnant at the time she had decided to leave the company, though it was possible that her heavy drinking and lifestyle had caused menstrual irregularities. She was just twenty-one when she joined the ship and was hardly in the mood to have an affair with Camb, who seems to have gone out of his way to be pleasant and helpful to everyone, and who was to be at her side frequently during the voyage.

There is no doubt that Camb was popular with most people, especially the ladies, who were completely bowled over by his charm and his looks, which were emphasised by his smart uniform. Even Gay, though preoccupied with her current worries, had taken to exchanging a few pleasantries with him over coffee or the occasional drink.

As the ship ploughed on through the shark-infested waters, the passengers began to relax more and more, until it became quite a common sight to see the first-class passengers mixing freely with the crew. On one of these occasions Gay got talking with James Camb, who asked her about her acting career, and then about Eric Boon, who was quite famous in those days. Later in the conversation, Gay let slip that she thought she might be pregnant and that she was in love with a man named Charles.

'If that's the position, why don't you marry the man?' Camb said, taking the role of a friend of long standing.

'It's not that easy,' Gay told him. 'There are problems. For one thing, he's already married.'

From then on, Camb got into the habit of seeing Gay every morning, bringing her a drink without even bothering to ask her what she wanted. This easy-going relationship developed with Gay continuing to talk about her stage career in Johannesburg. One evening she asked him to bring her a tray to her cabin. To a conceited man like Camb this could mean only one thing. Gay now wanted to have sex with him and was providing him with an excuse to visit her cabin.

Gay Gibson had had several lovers in her time and she was therefore far from being an innocent abroad, and for her to have given a man what amounted to free entry was to ask for trouble. Why did she ask for a tray to be taken to her late that evening, when she must have known that it could possibly lead to trouble?

By the time she went to her cabin that night she had drunk more than was good for her. Did that have any bearing on what happened later? It is difficult to say, as Camb may well have told a tissue of lies at his trial.

According to his account of what happened that evening, he had gone to her cabin only to find it unoccupied. He then went again to the cabin at 2 a.m. and found it still unoccupied. After he had waited around for some fifteen minutes, Gay had suddenly appeared, dressed in a yellow quilted dressing gown. He indicated the tray he had brought for her, but she no longer seemed interested in the snack which he had placed nearby. She settled back on her pillows and steadily drank from a glass of rum while she chatted to him as he sat on the edge of her bed. They had then indulged in a certain amount of love play, which had culminated in them having sex together.

As their intercourse reached its climax, Gay suddenly moaned and gripped his arms tightly, digging her nails into his flesh in what seemed to be the ecstasy of an approaching orgasm. To quote Camb's words, 'Suddenly her whole

279

body stiffened and her back arched in a violent spasm. She heaved a long, tired sigh, and her head lolled awkwardly to one side and her eyes opened wide and fixed me with a sightless stare.'

It was then that he became aware that there was something seriously amiss, and he spent the next twenty minutes vainly trying to revive her. It then began to dawn on him that she was in fact, dead, and that no smelling salts or resuscitation efforts would ever bring her back to life. What should he do now? The ship's doctor was near to hand, but to call him would mean the end of his career.

In a moment of surprising detachment, Camb suddenly decided that the only way for him to get out of this terrible situation was to get rid of the body. Having decided on this course of action, he lifted the body into a sitting position and manoeuvred it through the porthole above the bed. There was a loud splash as she entered the sea, but apart from that, nothing – such as a single cry from the look-out who might have seen the body go into the water.

It was at about this time that Steer, the deputy nightwatchman, noticed that both the red and green lights had gone on as he passed the indicator board in the first-class entrance hall. He had responded immediately to the ringing of the buzzer in the pantry, where he had been trying to fight off sleep. The two lights showing meant that both the steward and stewardess had been requested to attend cabin 126, which was occupied by Gay Gibson. Coming to the door of her cabin he knocked and tried to enter, only to have the door slammed in his face. The door then opened a few inches, and Steer just had time to hear

Camb say 'It's all right,' before the door closed once again.

How the lights had come on in the first place remains something of a mystery, though it was the contention of the prosecution at the trial that Gay Gibson had pressed the bell pushes while threshing around in her death throes, or that she had attempted to summon help to save her from Camb's unwanted advances. To this day, why and when they were pressed is still unknown. That she had summoned help does not really stand up under examination. Camb had been in the cabin for more than an hour before the lights came on, and it seems unlikely that he would have been that slow in making a pass. As for the prosecution's other argument, it is most unlikely that Gay pressed the bell pushes while fighting off Camb. Like so many things in this case, so many lies were told by Camb that it is difficult to get to the truth of anything. All we do know for certain is that the bell pushes were in perfect order on the night that Gay Gibson died. Apart from anything else, if Camb had known that the lights had come on, he had only to step outside the cabin for a few seconds and press in the bulbs to put them out.

At 7.30 the following morning, the cabin stewardess, Eileen Field, arrived at cabin 126 bearing the usual glass of orange juice for Gay Gibson. When there was no answer to her knock she went in and found the cabin empty. Looking briefly around her, she saw that the porthole was wide open, and that an early morning breeze was ruffling the curtains. She also noticed that the bed had been slept in. Seeing nothing untoward, she put down the orange juice and left.

It was not until after 9.30 a.m., after breakfast was finished, that Gay Gibson was found to be missing. A message was then broadcast over the ship's loudspeaker system, asking her to report immediately to the purser's office. When this brought no response, the captain then called for the ship to be searched from top to bottom, but again with negative results. The captain then ordered the vessel to be turned back, and the sea was searched for her. This was a forlorn hope at best, but the search lasted until around 7.30 p.m. when the ship then resumed its normal course.

Not until later in the day, after her possessions had been locked away for safe keeping, and a radio message sent to Scotland Yard, did Captain Patey begin questioning the crew. None of them was able to contribute anything which would throw light on Gay Gibson's disappearance. Camb's manner was suspicious and subdued, and Captain Patey immediately realised that he was concealing something. He said as much to Camb, who was wearing a long-sleeved shirt that day to hide the scratches that Gay had inflicted on him. After he had reluctantly agreed to be examined by Dr Griffiths, the ship's surgeon, he was allowed to leave.

Dr Griffiths then reported to Captain Patey that he had found a number of scratches on Camb's body, which he had claimed were the result of having rubbed himself too energetically with a coarse towel.

Nothing more was said to Camb, however, and he was allowed to continue with his duties until the ship reached Cowes Roads, where it was boarded by Detective Sergeant

Quinlan and Detective Constable Minden Plumley of the
Southampton police.

After searching Gay Gibson's cabin, they then interviewed Camb in the ship's smoking room. Quinlan opened
the proceedings by asking if they could see the scratches
that were on Camb's arms. He showed them to the two men
without demur, repeating his story of how they had been
self-inflicted by rubbing himself too hard with a rough
towel.

'We have reason to believe that you visited Gay Gibson's
cabin sometime about 3 a.m. on 18 October,' Quinlan
said. He then went on to ask Camb to accompany him to
Southampton police headquarters.

'That puts me in a tight spot—' Camb began.

Before he could say anything else, Quinlan interrupted
him. 'I suggest we carry on this conversation at the station.'
Camb was taken to police headquarters, where he was put
in the charge of Sergeant Gibbons, while the two officers
returned to the ship. Sergeant Gibbons was at great pains
to point out the seriousness of the position in which Camb
found himself. As he also said to him, there was now
evidence that Miss Gibson had been pushed through the
porthole. It therefore stood to reason that it was of the
utmost importance for Camb to show that he had had
nothing to do with her disappearance.

'Does that mean that I murdered her, and that I shall be
charged with her murder?' Camb asked him.

'I cannot say,' Gibbons said, truthfully enough. 'One
thing I do know. The time is fast approaching when a
decision will have to be made about you.'

That decision was not long in coming. The next morning

Quinlan strolled back into the police station. 'James Camb,' he said formally, 'I charge you with the wilful murder of Eileen Isabella Ronnie Gibson.'

'My God!' cried Camb. 'Is it as serious as that?'

Faced with the grim reality that he was about to go on trial for his life for the murder of Gay Gibson, Camb's self-assured, not to say cocky manner, had now completely crumbled. To give him credit, his first thoughts were of his wife and how she would be able to face up to the news when it was broken to her. As it happened, his wife took the news very badly, and she wrote to him, saying that she would never live with him again and wanted a divorce.

From the day of his arrest he was a broken man, and from that point onwards he began to age perceptibly.

The trial of James Camb opened at the Winchester Assizes on 18 March 1948, with Mr Justice Hilbery presiding over the case. The judge was considered to be a 'bloody awful judge to appear before if you were defending', to quote the words of someone who had been in the role of defending counsel before him. Even worse for the defendant was that the man taking the role of public prosecutor was G. D. Roberts KC, who was strongly in favour of capital punishment. More familiarly known as 'Khaki' Roberts, he had already made a formidable reputation for himself in the Nuremberg Trials only a couple of years earlier, when he had given the Nazi war criminals a hard time of it when they appeared in the dock. A shaggy bear of a man, he was liable to strike terror into the heart of anyone who came up against him, not least someone like Camb, who had a great deal to fear from his merciless cross-examination.

Fortunately for Camb, he had a good man defending him in Joshua Casswell KC, a well-known lawyer, who soon proved himself to be a worthy opponent to Roberts, who contended from the start that Camb had deliberately strangled Gay Gibson before pushing her through the porthole.

As was to be expected, much of the evidence hinged on the scratches that had been found on Camb's body. On this matter, the ship's surgeon, Dr Griffiths, who had been the only person to see them at an early stage, was listened to with particular interest. He described the nature of the scratches he had seen on Camb on the morning he had examined him.

'Would you say the scratches were made by convulsive gripping at the point of death?' Mr Casswell asked him.

'All I can say with certainty is that the scratches appear to have been made by a digging and drawing movement,' Dr Griffiths said.

In the end this line of questioning did not get Mr Casswell very far, as other witnesses came forward to say that the scratch marks were more consistent with a person struggling for their life while being strangled, while Dr Teare, the assistant pathologist and lecturer at St George's Hospital, London, stated that it was possible that death had resulted from natural causes. The upshot of all this is easily summarised: death could have occurred from strangulation, or death could have occurred from natural causes.

Throughout the trial, Camb cut a very poor figure in the dock, mostly because of the cold and callous way he described how he got rid of the body. His case was not helped by the way he was caught out lying time and time again, and by the fact that he never betrayed any sign of emotion as he told his story. If any man helped to dig his own grave in a trial in which he was fighting for his life, it was James Camb.

They were still going on about the scratches found on Camb on the second day of the trial. In the course of his examination of Dr Griffiths, Mr Casswell asked him, while showing him a photograph of the scratches, 'Are they consistent with the man's arms being gripped tightly and then released?'

'Yes,' Dr Griffiths said simply.

Continuing with his efforts to prove that his client had not throttled Gay Gibson before pushing her body through the porthole, he then asked Griffiths a few more questions and then left the floor to Roberts, who was equally determined to prove that Camb *had* murdered her before getting rid of the body. And so it went on, with each of the KCs striving to score points over his opponent.

There was also a great deal of argument about some bloodstains that had been found on the sheet, as were a number of other stains which were established as being urine stains that had come from Miss Gibson. In this matter, Roberts wasted no time in coming to the point in his examination of Dr Teare. 'In death by strangulation is any discharge of blood from the victim likely?' he asked.

Dr Teare agreed that it was. Roberts then asked him if suffocation by a pillow would bring on internal bleeding.

'I would not expect it, though it might occur,' Teare said.

When the time came for Mr Casswell to examine Dr Teare on this point, the doctor said, 'I was not aware that urine had been found on the sheets. In my experience, death from asphyxia in particular, which includes death by strangulation, is frequently associated with terminal urination.'

It was not the sort of answer that Casswell had been looking for, and he therefore let the matter drop. Mr Roberts, however, did not let the matter rest at that. 'Now that you know the defence have ascertained the presence of urine on the sheets, does that strengthen your view as to whether death in this case was from strangulation?'

'It does.'

In his summing up, Roberts brought up two points that the jury could understand and appreciate. In the course of the trial it came to light that Miss Gibson had been in possession of a Dutch cap at the time Camb had come to her cabin. If they had sex together by mutual consent, why had she not used it? Secondly, Roberts declared, 'If she had died a natural death in his arms as he now says she did, would it not have been easier for him to slip unobserved from her cabin, and then the girl would have been found in her bed, sleeping her last sleep, having died a natural death, a fact that any medical man could have established in a couple of minutes?'

Of course, as she believed she was already pregnant, using a contraceptive would have been unnecessary, but no one seems to have considered this point.

When it came to Casswell's summing up, he put the facts of the case as he saw them quietly and effectively, though he was not enjoying the best of health at the time. 'He is charged with having murdered that girl, and it is for the prosecution to prove beyond all doubt that he did murder her . . .' He then put forward his case for the defence, which was as fine a piece of detailed evidence as had ever been heard in that courtroom.

It was not enough. On 24 March 1948, the jury went out to consider the case and returned within forty-five minutes to give their verdict, in which they found Camb guilty of the murder of Gay Gibson.

Camb seemed stunned by the verdict. Throughout the trial he had maintained a level of exceptional coolness which could have been achieved if he was convinced throughout that he would be declared innocent. Brought to his feet, he stood there swaying in his tracks as he listened to the clerk of the court.

'James Camb, you stand convicted of murder. Have you anything to say why the court should not give judgement of death according to law?'

'My Lord, at the opening of this case, I was asked to plead guilty or not guilty,' Camb said in a quavering voice. 'I pleaded not guilty, and I repeat that statement now.'

Mr Justice Hilbery passed the sentence of death on him, and Camb shuffled from the court, now a completely broken man.

Camb escaped the executioner because the House of Commons was then debating an amendment to the new Criminal Justice Bill, and Camb was one of the lucky few who were spared, and he was sentenced to life imprisonment instead.

But this was far from being the end of the story. After serving out some of his sentence in Wakefield Prison he was sent to Parkhurst Prison on the Isle of Wight, where he became a model prisoner. In December 1948 his wife legally changed her name to McCombie, and soon afterwards married a clerk who worked for the solicitor who had represented Camb.

He was finally paroled in 1959, by which time the years were beginning to take their toll on him. In 1967 he was convicted of making sexual advances to a thirteen-year-old girl, for which he had the incredible luck of getting away with nothing more than being put on probation for two years. Soon afterwards he was at it again, this time with three schoolgirls while he was working at the Waverley Castle Hotel in Melrose, Scotland. One evening he had followed one of the girls, who was only ten, had locked the door of the hotel room behind them, and had then proceeded to push her on to the bed, and had begun to kiss and fondle her, until he heard someone in the corridor, when he abruptly got up and left. He had then gone into another room along the corridor, where two eleven-year-old girls were sleeping. He kissed one of them and was preparing to make further sexual advances, only to stop as soon as the girl had made it clear to him that she wanted no part whatsoever in what Camb was planning to do next. This time he was not so lucky as he had been on previous occasions. His licence was revoked and he was sent to prison to serve out the rest of his sentence.

He spent the next twelve years in prison and was finally released in 1978 and got himself a job at the Jester's public house, where he died suddenly of a heart attack on Saturday 7 July 1979. He was sixty-two.

Did Camb really murder Gay Gibson, or did she have a heart attack in the middle of the sexual act, as Camb always maintained until the day of his death?

Let us examine the facts. In the first place she was not in

the best of health at the time, though her mother claimed that she was. She was subject to fainting fits, and there had been that occasion when she was discovered by an ATS officer, sweating profusely and in a state of shock. She had been taken to the Casualty Receiving Station, and by the next morning she had recovered. She admitted later to the ATS officer that such attacks were not unknown to her.

When she had taken up the stage as a professional career, there was some talk of a heart condition because of the frequency of those curious attacks. She also had some sort of bronchial condition, and was always clearing her throat and spitting phlegm into her handkerchief. None of these things seem to have been serious in themselves, but they do not add up to a picture of someone who was in perfect health.

It was the prosecution's argument that she had been murdered by Camb while he was trying to have sex with her. Before the bell pushes had been pressed Camb had already been with Gay Gibson for the best part of an hour. What then was Miss Gibson doing all that time, unless it was indulging in love play and then sexual intercourse, when she had probably pushed the bells by accident?

The only stumbling block to this theory is why had she not fitted herself with the Dutch cap which was in her luggage, since she knew Camb was visiting her that night? On the other hand, she could have merely said to herself 'to hell with it', and just not bothered, particularly as she suspected she was pregnant.

It is my conviction that Camb, worthless though he was, and far too obsessed with sex for his own good, was innocent of the murder of Gay Gibson. This view was shared by a number of people, including Joshua Casswell, who so ably defended him in the face of a hostile judge and a public prosecutor who was all for capital punishment.

A
DRUNKEN KILLER

Anyone meeting nineteen-year-old Michael Douglas Dowdall for the first time could have been forgiven if they had taken him to be just like any young man of his social background. He was born in 1940, the son of an army captain who had been killed in the war in 1943, when his mother looked after him until she, too, died suddenly, leaving him to be brought up by an aunt in Wales from the age of eight. When he was eighteen he had joined the Welsh Guards. By then he had grown up to be a pleasant-looking young man whose only fault seemed to be that he liked to drink too much, a common enough failing in lads of his age, to impress their drinking companions.

Though to his drinking mates he was merely an agreeable, if somewhat garrulous bar room companion, in reality Dowdall was a brooding young man, a highly dangerous person who was quite capable of the most horrific acts of violence whenever he had had too much to drink. While in a state of intoxication he had already viciously attacked and nearly strangled to death a woman who had been unwise enough to take him to her flat in

Fulham. In December of 1958 he had actually murdered a prostitute named Veronica Murray in her flat in Kilburn. On that occasion the police had tried to trace the murderer, but as they knew little or nothing about him, they had to abandon their search. That had been nearly a year ago, and they still had no idea of who the murderer was. Fortunately, however, the woman whom Dowdall had attacked previously in Fulham, had gone to the police and told them how she had nearly been strangled with one of her own silk stockings. With that information the police felt that the murderer of Veronica Murray was probably the same man, and therefore clearly a sex maniac who would almost certainly strike again.

As luck would have it, they also learned from the woman who had lived to tell the tale after the assault on her, that the attacker had possessed an unusual cigarette lighter marked 'The Texas Gulf Sulphur Company'. Obtaining a photograph of their lighter from the Texas Gulf Sulphur Company, they arranged for it to be published in the national press, where it was seen by a Welsh Guardsman who got in touch with the police through his commanding officer. The Guardsman reported that such a lighter had been in the possession of Dowdall. Dowdall was brought to London where he was interviewed by Detective Chief Inspector Acott at Chelsea police station.

After openly admitting to a number of robberies, Dowdall said: 'I want to tell you now about something I think is serious. It has been worrying me for nearly a year.' With Acott taking down every word he said, Dowdall told how he had gone to London just before Christmas 1958, when he had picked up a prostitute. She had called a taxi and they had gone to her flat in Kilburn. As soon as he heard the address, Acott knew that they were talking about Veronica Murray.

'We quarrelled, and she called me a little Welsh bastard,' Dowdall said with some emotion. 'I then threw a vase at her, and we continued to go for each other until I finally left to spend the night at the Union Jack Club for the Forces. When I awoke the next morning it was to find my suit and hands were covered with blood. A couple of days afterwards I read in the newspapers that a prostitute had been found murdered in Kilburn. I knew then that I had murdered the woman.'

'What about the woman in Fulham?' Acott prompted him.

'I met her celebrating her birthday in the West End.' Dowdall then described how they had gone to her flat, where he tried to have sex with her. 'She refused, when we had a violent row. I don't remember much more of what happened that night, except that I tore off some of her clothes. Then I left, taking some money and a bottle of whisky with me.'

Dowdall was charged with Veronica Murray's murder and was put on trial at the Old Bailey in January 1960. Mr Morton, acting for the Crown, did not mince his words in his opening speech to the jury. 'You might as well reconcile yourselves to the facts; this is a horrible murder.' He then outlined the case to the jury. When he had finished, it was left to Mr Desmond Trenner, acting for the defence, to prove that his client had been justified in pleading not guilty to murder, putting forward the plea of diminished responsibility.

295

Apart from being a troublemaker at school from the very early age of six, he had grown up in the stifling confines of a typical Welsh town, under the guidance of his aunt, who tried to give him some stability in life. Her efforts were wasted on Dowdall, who continued to be quite uncontrollable and often destructive, until the age of eighteen, when he had joined the Welsh Guards. No longer was he the bane of the lives of his teachers and social workers, the only problem Dowdall now had was in trying to hold his own with his drinking companions. His answer to that was to drink more than anyone else. It was nothing for him to drink four half pints of gin in one drinking session.

The question of Dowdall's drinking habits was brought up at the trial when Mr Justice Donovan asked Sergeant Peter Clotworthy if he did not feel it incumbent upon him to stop him drinking half a pint of gin in a tankard at one go. 'Did you feel no responsibility for him?' the judge asked.

'Not while he was out of barracks,' Clotworthy said.

On another occasion during the trial, Dowdall's defence counsel asked, 'After drinking four half pints of gin, did he walk away from the bar?'

'No. He was carried out,' he was told.

And so it had gone on, with question after question being fired at various witnesses, who all agreed that Dowdall had been seen drinking far too much, but no one had ever done anything to try and stop him.

All this seemed to indicate that a verdict of murder would be given in this case – that was until Dr Brisby took the stand.

'Tell me,' said Mr Morton. 'Could a boy of eighteen drink a bottle of gin in two hours?'

'He could,' replied Dr Brisby, 'but it would have the most dire results.'

A Dr A. D. Leigh, the psychiatrist from Bethlehem Hospital was then summoned to the stand. 'I have examined Dowdall,' he announced. 'It is my opinion that he is a psychopath and a sexual pervert. He certainly has all the characteristics of one, which are aggressiveness, impulsiveness, lying, sexual perversion and often alcoholism.'

If nothing else, these latter witnesses had made it obvious that Dowdall would no longer be charged with murder, but merely with the lesser crime of manslaughter.

This indeed proved to be so. When the jury returned after three hours of deliberation, it was to announce they found Dowdall guilty of the manslaughter of Veronica Murray, and not guilty of murder, on the grounds of diminished responsibility. The final words on the case belonged to Mr Justice Donovan, who directly addressed Dowdall: 'It would clearly be unsafe to impose on you a sentence of a fixed term of years, at the end of which you would be set free. The sentence must therefore be one which will enable the authorities to detain you until they are satisfied that you can safely mingle with your fellow creatures once again.'

THE
RELUCTANT LOVER

Flying Officer William James Croft was stationed at the RAF camp at Predannack in Cornwall, when he met a Welsh Corporal in the WAAF named Joan Nora Lewis. She was an attractive young woman, and in no time at all they had become deeply involved with each other, sleeping together in one of the local inns whenever they could. Despite their passion for each other, it was not altogether a happy situation for either of them. Croft was a married man with two children. According to Croft, he was trapped in a loveless marriage which he claimed he had only held together for the sake of the children. His conversations with Joan Lewis were frequently peppered with such wistful phrases as 'If only I was not married, etc.', the truth of the matter being that he did not really want to get a divorce at all, and even if he had submitted a petition it would have been most unlikely that it would have been granted.

As was inevitable, it was only a matter of time before their affair came to the attention of the WAAF authorities and his station commander. It was decided that Joan Lewis was to be transferred to a station in Devon, to which she reluctantly agreed, while Croft, perhaps realising that the situation was in fact getting well out of hand, saw that the suggested posting was for the best.

It was at about this time that Croft started talking about a suicide pact, either by jumping over a cliff or by shooting. For an incurable romantic like Joan Lewis, who already saw the two of them as star-crossed lovers, the idea of a suicide pact soon became irresistible, especially as she was by now so much in love with Croft that to imagine any sort of life without him was impossible.

It is difficult for anyone to know what exactly was in Croft's mind when they met on that summer evening to go through with their suicide pact. It would seem that having engineered himself into an impossible situation, he was hoping against hope that nothing would come of the suicide pact when it was time to carry it out. Perhaps he even saw himself as Joan Lewis saw him – as a lover who was prepared to die with her rather than lose her for all time. All that anyone can do is to relate the facts as they were presented to the police by Croft.

Croft's story was that they had made their way to a nearby summerhouse. Placing the gun on his lap, he arranged with the girl that whoever made the first movement would kill their partner and then shoot themselves. According to Croft he had fallen asleep when he felt the gun being taken from his lap, after which there was the sound of a shot. Fully awake now, he turned and found Joan Lewis gasping in agony beside him.

'It's hurting me,' she gasped, clasping her breast. 'I need help.'

Croft hurried off for help, but he had only gone a few

yards when there was the sound of another shot. He hurried back to the summerhouse, where he found the girl dead. He had then tried to kill himself but found he was unable to bring himself to pull the trigger. He then phoned the duty officer and told him that he had killed Joan Lewis. Later, however, when he was being examined by the police, he changed his story and denied emphatically that he had killed her.

Dr Dennis Hocking, a well-known local pathologist, was called in to give his expert opinion. 'My opinion is that she fired neither of the shots,' he announced. 'After the first shot she lived for a few minutes before she was killed by the second shot through the head.'

After Dr Hocking's statement, what had only seemed to be the tragic aftermath of a doomed love affair had now become a murder case, with Croft as the suspect.

He was arrested and put on trial at Winchester Assizes, where his case was defended by Mr Humphrey Edwards KC, who vainly tried to convince the jury that the victim had killed herself. It was his contention that she had held the heavy service weapon while bringing it up to her chest. She had then fired it, when the gun had fallen on to the floor and discharged the second bullet to her head. However, Dr Hocking's findings were that the bullet was aimed at her heart, but completely missed it, fracturing a rib, and, continuing its entry backwards, had emerged under her armpit and severely damaged the muscle used to raise her arm. The second shot, the one that killed her, entered the skull above her left eye and emerged in front of the right ear. The skin around the bullet wound was entirely free of burn marks, and the bullet was, in the opinion of Dr

Hocking, fired from some eighteen inches away. All this seemed to make Mr Humphrey Edwards' theory rather impossible, and the jury chose to ignore it.

Throughout the trial Croft created an unfavourable impression with the jury. He again reverted to his story of a suicide pact that had gone wrong, and the way he told it did nothing to endear him to any of his listeners, especially when it came to pulling the trigger on himself. Not that it doesn't take a great deal of courage to pull the trigger on oneself, particularly if there is an underlying reluctance in the first place! The truth of the matter, one suspects, was that Croft had got into a situation from which he could not extricate himself. He had shown throughout that he was an extremely weak character, who had allowed himself to be carried along by events until it was too late for him to do anything about it. He had then finally shot Joan Lewis, probably intending to kill himself afterwards, only to find he could not pull the trigger, as he freely admitted.

Dennis Hocking, who lived locally, and was called in on the case from the very beginning, states in his book *Bodies and Crimes*, that it was probably a suicide pact that went hideously wrong, as Croft stated himself at his trial. When it came to it, however, Hocking's evidence at the trial did not help Croft. 'In my experience women don't like to dispose of themselves in actual fact by using a gun,' Hocking told the court. 'It is just possible – though I don't think it happened – that the girl fired the revolver into her chest. She lived for a few minutes after the first shot had been fired, and was killed by the second shot through the head.'

Mr Humphrey Edwards KC, acting for the defence, and

302

who happened to be something of a firearms expert himself, did his best for his client by putting on a spectacular display in mime in trying to prove that the girl herself had fired both shots.

None of this impressed the jury, who brought in a verdict of guilty, and Croft was sentenced to be hanged by Mr Justice Humphries. Croft's appeal was also denied, but eventually his sentence was commuted to one of life imprisonment.

BIBLIOGRAPHY

Apart from the use of a number of press reports, many books have been consulted in the writing of this collection of true murder cases, and I hereby acknowledge them with my thanks. They are as follows:

Thomas Henry Allaway, *The Pleasures of Murder*, Jonathan Goodman, Allison & Busby, 1983

Amelia Archer, *Murder, Mayhem and Mystery*, Alan Hynd, A. S. Barnes & Co., 1958

Kenneth Barlow, *Famous Criminal Cases No. 5*, Leonard Gribble, Allan Wingate, 1958

Charles Becker, *Against the Evidence*, Andy Logan, The McCall Publishing Co., 1970

Reginald Sidney Buckfield, *The Trial of Reg. Buckfield*, C. E. Bechhoffer Roberts, Jarrolds, 1944

Unknown, *The Murder Club: Lieutenant Chevis*, devised and edited by Brian Lane, Harrap Ltd, 1988

James Camb, *The Porthole Murder Case*, Denis Herbstein, Hodder & Stoughton, 1991

James Camb, *The Trial of James Camb. Notable British Trials Series No. 71*, edited by Geoffrey Clark, Wm. Hodge & Co. Ltd, 1949

William James Croft, *Bodies and Crimes*, Dr F. D. M. Hocking, The Book Guild Ltd, 1992

Harry Dobkin, *Clues that Spelled Guilty*, Leonard Gribble, John Long, 1961

Michael Douglas Dowdall, *Famous Criminal Cases No. 6*, Leonard Gribble, Odhams Press Ltd, 1960

Mick Emmett-Dunne, *Famous Criminal Cases No. 3*, Leonard Gribble, Allan Wingate, 1956

Robert Erler, *Murder America*, Jay Robert Nash, Harrap Ltd, 1981

Neville Heath, *The Murders of the Black Museum*, Gordon Honeycombe, Hutchinson, 1982

Arthur Heys, *Forty Years of Murder*, Keith Simpson, Harrap Ltd, 1978

Adolph Hofrichter, *Crime on the Continent*, Horace Wyndham, Thornton Butterworth, 1938

Karl Gustav Hulten and Elizabeth Maud Jones, *The Murder and the Trial*, Edgar Lustgarten, Odhams Press Ltd, 1960

Genene Ann Jones, *Encyclopaedia of Modern Murder*, Colin Wilson and Donald Seaman, Book Club Associates, 1983

Winnie Ruth Judd, *Los Angeles Murders*, edited by Craig Rice Duell, Sloan & Pearce Inc., 1947

Edward Leonski, *Crime Chemist*, Alan Dower, John Long Ltd, 1965

Wayne Lonergan, *A Chair for Wayne Lonergan*, Hamilton Darby Perry, The Macmillan Company, NY, 1972

Bertie Manton, *Forty Years of Murder*, Keith Simpson, Harrap Ltd, 1978

Marcus Marymont, *Famous Criminal Cases No. 3*, Rupert Furneaux, Allan Wingate, 1956

John Donald Merrett, *Portrait of a Bad Man*, Tom Tullett, Evans Bros., 1956

Dale Pierre and William Andrews, *Victim*, Gary Kinder, Delacorte Press, NY, 1982

James Ronald Robertson, *World Encyclopedia of 20th Century Murder*, J. Robert Nash, Headline, 1992

August Sangret, *The Crime Doctors*, Robert Jackson, Frederick Muller Ltd, 1966

Jane Toppan, *Encyclopedia of Serial Killers*, Brian Lane and Wilfred Gregg, Headline, 1992

INDEX

311